DOUBLE YOUR LEARNING POWER

Sound advice to help you improve the quality of your memory.

DOUBLE YOUR LEARNING POWER

Master the Techniques of Successful Memory and Recall

by

GEOFFREY A. DUDLEY

THORSONS PUBLISHING GROUP

This edition first published January 1986
Second Impression August 1986

British Library Cataloguing in Publication Data

Dudley, Geoffrey A.
Double your learning power: master the
techniques of successful memory and recall.
Rev. expanded and reset ed.
1. Mnemonics
I. Title   II. Dudley, Geoffrey A. Increase
your learning power
153.1'4   BF385

ISBN 0-7225-1211-2

*Published by Thorsons Publishers Limited,
Wellingborough, Northamptonshire, NN8 2RQ, England*

Printed in Great Britain by
Richard Clay Limited, Bungay, Suffolk

5   7   9   10   8   6

TO NICHOLA, DARREN,
MICHAEL AND JONATHAN

ACKNOWLEDGEMENTS

My thanks are due to Robert D. Heap, who very kindly agreed to write a Foreword to this book.

Contents

		Page
Foreword		9
Preface		11
Chapter		
1.	What is Memory?	15
2.	Why We Forget	34
3.	How to Remember	60
4.	Mnemonics for Learning Power	108
5.	The Technique of Passing Exams	132
6.	How to Forget	150
7.	Summary of Practical Hints	156
	Appendix: How to Read Faster	173
	References	179
	Select Bibliography	187
	Index	191

Foreword

Do you often forget the very things you want to remember? Are you embarrassed in business and social life by being unable to recall the names of people you have met before? Do you have difficulty in remembering what you read? Do telephone numbers, addresses, and figures slip your mind?

Few things can hold you back so much as an exasperating habit of forgetfulness.

A good memory is worth money in any business or profession. The most efficient and successful men and women are those who *can* remember, instantly and accurately, whatever they have filed away in their mental 'card indexes'.

They talk more intelligently; they are more interesting and more convincing. They have the facts and figures 'on the tips of their tongues' to back up every idea, every proposal, every discussion. No wonder they make the best executives, the most competent employees!

And socially they are the most delightful companions because they have a wealth of reliable conversational knowledge that puts them at ease in any company.

Yet keep in mind this one important fact: No one was ever *born* with a good memory. True, some people do have unusually good memories, while others seem to be natural 'forgetters'. But the former have *acquired* their retentive minds. By properly developing it, they have discovered what the mind is capable of.

Strengthening your memory is not a difficult task at all. If you have trouble in remembering something, help is at hand. Learning is one of the problems that is receiving the most intensive study by psychologists at the present time. Even though the problem is by no means completely solved, practical conclusions can be drawn from what is already known.

This is what Geoffrey Dudley has set himself to do in his instructive book. Its practical interest lies in the discovery of ways and means of *learning more efficiently.* In the simplest terms, the practical problem of learning is to get something into our heads so that it will stay there. We want to impress something on our mind in such a way that it will be available whenever we need it. When the knowledge or skill is at our fingertips, we can fairly claim that we have learned it.

In following the advice offered in this book you are putting yourself in the hands of an author with long experience of training students. For many years he has directed the home-study courses conducted by the Company founded by my father. As its present Chairman and Managing Director, I can from my own knowledge of Geoffrey Dudley's work recommend his book as deserving the close attention of all who wish to solve the common problem of retaining what they learn.

ROBERT D. HEAP
Marple,
Cheshire.

Preface

This book is different from other books on learning and memory in several ways. First of all, it does not subscribe to the belief that there is such a thing as memory. A memory is not something that we possess; the word does not correspond to any faculty in the mind. Rather, remembering is something that we do or that the brain does. 'Memory' is postulated to account for the fact that we remember. This fact is the only evidence for its existence. This book, therefore, deals directly with what we do, i.e., remember, not indirectly with something, i.e., memory, which is supposed to make that activity possible.

Secondly, this book does not subscribe to the belief that memory can be improved. This is not the same thing as saying that we cannot remember better. We can remember better but it is not because our memory can be improved; it is because we can improve our methods of memorizing and recalling. No scientific evidence is so far available which would suggest that there is any way of improving the brain's sheer power of retaining what is memorized. Indeed, there is plenty of evidence that as we grow older this power of retention actually deteriorates.

Thirdly, this is not a book for those who like advice unsupported by scientific evidence. In writing it we have not sat down and indulged in theorizing about how we remember. We have gone to those who have actually studied the ways in which people remember, i.e., the psychologists who have conducted laboratory experiments on the subject. And plenty of experiments have been conducted in this field — enough, I believe, to justify making those findings more widely known to the general public. For over thirty-five years the author has combed the research literature and textbooks for information on what psychologists have discovered about memory. This book is the result.

If there are any mistakes or shortcomings in it, the author accepts full responsibility and would be grateful to have them pointed out to him. Any credit for the practical value of what is discussed herein, however, should go to others. It belongs to the research psychologists who have conducted careful and painstaking experiments to find out exactly how people remember and what conditions favour their remembering better.

Of course, it would be fallacious to suppose that the last word has been said on this subject. But the author has striven to make the information contained in these chapters as up to date as possible. If he has missed out any important research findings that should have been included, or has failed to draw any practical conclusion that seems justified, he offers his sincere apologies for it.

The purpose of this book, then, is twofold: to acquaint the reader with what psychologists have discovered about learning, remembering and forgetting, and to suggest practical ways of making use of that knowledge.

It contains no magical formula for becoming a mental prodigy. It does not purport to show you how to develop a 'photographic memory'. It offers no guarantee that with its aid you will win a big prize on a TV quiz show. Nor does it advance any claim to have discovered some occult method of memory training of which psychology is still ignorant. It is written for sensible men and women who recognize that there are limits to what we can or should learn and remember, but who share the author's view that these limits need not be too cramping nor too insurmountable.

Much of our learning is dependent upon the kind of motivation which lies behind our behaviour. By motivation we mean those persistent conditions within ourselves which move us to act.

Some controversy exists about whether these motives are innate or whether they are derived from experience. Psychologists who subscribe to the 'innate' view list various instincts as the primary sources of behaviour. Some examples of these instincts are: sex, hunger, curiosity, aggressiveness, etc. Other psychologists believe that the individual learns to act as he does in certain situations as a result of his early childhood training.

At present this controversy cannot be settled to the satisfaction of both schools. For the time being the most reasonable attitude to take is that of supposing that both innate drives and upbringing contribute determinants of our behaviour, including our behaviour in learning situations.

Such a view is consistent with the fact that individuals differ in the degree and range of their motivation. Some students will learn out of love of the subject-matter itself, while others need some ulterior purpose to assist them; they need to be able to find in their learning some practical value or some way of furthering their personal ambitions. The task of the school is to foster both types of motivation and to provide the proper conditions that will encourage both types of learners.

We have spoken so far of motives which are conscious, but psychoanalysis has also accustomed us to think in terms of unconscious motivation. Unconscious motives can both assist and interfere with learning. Probably the latter type of situation is the more common. The type of child who is referred to the Child Guidance Clinic is likely to be the one in whom unconscious motives arising from family problems, insecurity, emotional conflicts, etc., are interfering with the mastery of school subjects. Such children can be greatly helped by being encouraged to 'work off' their repressed feelings in various ways, e.g. finger painting, play therapy, etc. When this has been done the child can return to the school and make normal progress in his or her studies.

We see, then, that motivation exerts an important influence upon success and failure in studies. It can, without doubt, make a vast difference to the amount learned and how well it is learned. In whatever we try to learn, therefore, we should make an effort to link it to some motive which is prominent in our lives. If you are studying something which you don't see the need of, try to find in it some advantage which will give you a motive for doing your best at it. The good teacher is the one who can help his pupils to tie up the school subjects with their motives in this way.

The author's main debt is to the psychologists who have undertaken the research upon which this book relies heavily. I am grateful for the privilege of drawing upon the studies which are cited in these pages. I hope that those responsible for them will feel that the debt has been repaid if this book succeeds in making their findings known to a wider section of the public.

The cases cited in the text have been drawn from the author's forty years' experience as a psychological consultant. The author must express his deep appreciation and gratitude to those persons upon whose experiences he has drawn in this way. He would not have presumed to offer his advice to others had not those who have used it proved its value for themselves.

The author can ask no better reward than that the reader may be encouraged to use the practical hints which others have used, and by reading these pages may achieve a better understanding of the functions of remembering and forgetting.

'Memory,' says Dr Erwin Dunlop, 'is like Janus, the god of the new year. It faces backward to the past, relates the past to the present, and from this basis it determines our future. We are what we are, because we remember. Memory is the instrument that preserves the continuity of our experience, and thus shapes our whole personality.'[1]

GEOFFREY A. DUDLEY
Handforth,
Cheshire.

1.

What is Memory?

The 'Thingummybob' Principle

As you read the opening words of this chapter, an image of what you read is being formed in your mind. In fact, all the things you experience with your senses are stored as mental images. These mental images can be revived because *every experience that we undergo is recorded in the brain and nervous system.* That is why we are able to remember our experiences.

This basic fact of mental life, upon which both remembering and forgetting depend, was called by the American psychologist William James the '*thingummybob' principle.*

Remembering, then, means *attending to a mental image which has been determined by a past experience.* It is the power to retain knowledge in the mind, to recall impressions of past events. The past is brought into the present by means of mental images of the things perceived by the sense organs.

The ideas of memory may originate in actual experiences or in ideas of such experiences. That is to say, I can remember an experience and I can also remember having remembered it.

In actual practice a group of similar experiences is revived as often as a single past experience. For example, when we remember what a bicycle looks like, we may not remember a particular bicycle. Rather we have a memory image compounded of the memory images of many bicycles which we have seen.

If, as we have said, remembering depends upon images, how does it differ from imagination and thinking? Images play a part in these mental activities too. The difference is one of function, not of the material of which the images are composed. The function of images in memory is to represent past experiences. In imagination the images relate to what is thought of as occurring in the future.

Past experience, too, is made use of in thinking. Whereas remembering is a direct use of what has been learned, thinking is an indirect use. Remembering is repeating something previously experienced, while thinking is doing something partly original.

What makes it possible for us to remember at all? The exact nature of the process of retention is uncertain. But an answer to the question must be sought in the brain, the physical organ of the mind that experiences.

In recent years there has been a renewal of interest in finding a physiological basis for the phenomena of memory.

Three theories of how the mental image is stored in the brain hold the field. One is that an experience, say, a conversation, lays down an actual physical impression in the brain structure. Reactivation of this impression, which is called a memory trace, is held to account for subsequent recall of what was said in the conversation.

A later view (although not the latest) is that memories are stored in the form of patterns of electrical impulses. These have no fixed location in any particular area of the brain, but they establish permanent records of our experiences in the networks of nerve cells.

These earlier theories may be contrasted with the latest theory, which is chemical in nature. The chemical factor involved may be the activity of protein molecules. Proteins are organic compounds forming a vital part of all living organisms. It has been found that they are rapidly synthesized in nerve cells by RNA (ribonucleic acid), which may modify brain cells so that they can store information.

There are two pieces of evidence in support of this. Hyden, who dissected the brains of rats after they had been trained, found that proteins produced by RNA had increased in amount and changed in shape and activity. Secondly, mice trained to perform a task forgot the task when given an antibiotic which stops the production of proteins. [2]

There are arguments both for and against all three views. For example, great as the number of brain cells is, it is nevertheless limited. During the course of an average lifetime a person receives far more impressions than could possibly be stored in the brain if we allow only one impression per cell. The number of brain cells has been calculated as being in the region of 10 billion. On the other hand, in an average lifetime the brain might have to store up to 15 trillion bits of information. This necessitates some arrangement which will make the storage possible. It gives point to the theory which explains the laying down of memory images in terms of changes in the protein structure of the cell.

This objection to the possibility of the brain's accommodating all the impressions a person receives takes into account the time he spends asleep. Then presumably he receives no stimulation from the outside world, although even this view has now been seriously questioned.

Recent research has also discovered two kinds of storage: temporary (short-term) and permanent (long-term). During temporary storage an impression is liable to be erased, although even when in permanent storage, it can still be temporarily forgotten. After about an hour, the memory is either erased or transferred to permanent storage. It is the latter which involves changes in the amount and composition of the protein molecules in the brain cells. Studies suggest, in fact, that short-term memory is electrical, long-term is chemical.

The chemical view of the nature of memory is, however, on less firm ground than the electrical. McConnell gave flatworms an electric shock preceded by a bright light. Having learned to respond to the light in anticipation of the shock, they were then ground up and fed to other flatworms. McConnell found that the second group responded to the light without having been trained to do so. He argued that the memory of the learning experience was transferred chemically from one set of worms to the other. [3]

The validity of McConnell's finding is uncertain because other researchers have been unable to repeat his experiment. They found it impossible to condition the worms or to obtain transfer of the 'memory' in the way that McConnell claimed. The academic world remained sceptical of the result and, as Barry Singer remarks in *Science and the Paranormal*, circulated jokes about grinding up older professors and feeding them to younger ones.

The electrical activity of the brain may play a part in the retrieval of memories. 'Brainwaves', as this activity is commonly known, are poorly organized in early infancy, and this may explain why we can recall virtually nothing from that period of life.

At present it is impossible to decide among the above views. It may even be that all three are true and that there are memories of three types: those laid down in a particular area of the brain, those existing as patterns of electrical stimulation, and those represented by protein activity. If, throughout this book, we continue to refer to memory traces, we do so only for the sake of brevity of description. The reader should not take this to mean that the issue has been settled in favour of the trace theory as against the other two.

The ability to remember anything at all, then, is an inherent biological condition of nature.

Obviously, different people are differently endowed in this respect, but few people make the fullest use of what nature has given them. Our aim is to help you remember but to do it within the limits imposed by nature. We do not set ourselves the impossible task of transcending those limits.

'Faculty' Psychology

Whatever the truth, one thing is clear. There is no such thing as 'the memory'. People often complain: 'I find great difficulty in remembering what I read. I want you to tell me how to train the memory.' One can understand the need that prompts such a request, but psychologists are not very fond of referring to *the* memory.

There are several reasons for this. One is that to speak of the memory suggests that it is a thing. It creates a picture of there being in the head a little box into which we pop our memories and from which they pop out again. This is, of course, not true.

Secondly, it suggests that if there were such a thing as the memory we should have only one of it. This, too, is not true. The truth is that we have different memories for different kinds of material. In the same person some of these memories may be good and others not so good. For example, a man said: 'I have an excellent memory for names and faces, but I find it difficult to memorize facts connected with my professional accountancy studies.'

Another man said: 'My memory for knowledge directly connected with my job and my hobby is very good. The names of people, however, are an entirely different matter and most of the time I cannot remember them.'

Thirdly, memory is not really something static. It is a dynamic process or mental activity; it is something that a person does, not something that he possesses. It would be better to say that he remembers than that he has a memory or memories.

The idea of there being a memory, however, is so firmly rooted that we will use it for the sake of convenience. As we do it should be borne in mind that we are thinking of the activity of remembering, not of the possession of a faculty of memory.

To speak of the memory harks back to a past tradition in psychology, when it was fashionable to believe in what are known as mental faculties. 'Faculty' psychology, which sponsored this view, taught that there exists a number of discrete mental faculties, each of which is responsible for all mental acts of a particular kind. For example, all acts of remembering were held to be due to the existence of a faculty of memory; all acts of willing to a faculty of will. Other 'faculties' were reason, imagination, perception, judgement, etc.

This view belongs to the era when psychology was called 'mental philosophy' — an old-fashioned term no longer in use. Once very popular, faculty psychology is now discredited. The evidence against it is provided by such observations as that in ageing people a very poor memory for recent events may coexist with an excellent one for events of the distant past. Obviously, then, there cannot be a general faculty of memory which is responsible for both kinds of remembering.

The point that memory is not a single faculty may be illustrated from the life of a certain professor of medicine. We are told that as a young man he had such a remarkable memory that he could glance over a page of Shakespeare selected at random and then repeat it word for word. Yet it was not unusual for him to forget to put on his collar and tie or jacket when he left home to lecture to his students.

In this case an excellent memory for Shakespeare coexisted with a very poor memory for the ordinary details of life. The professor was, in fact, absent-minded only for certain things. This he could not have been if all his memory activities had been governed by the work of a single 'faculty'.

A person may acquire marvellous memory power for knowledge gained along a certain line and yet be hopelessly inadequate in recalling items unconnected with his particular interest. Someone may readily memorize and recall facts, but have little success in remembering figures and dates. Another person may remember faces more easily than he can recall tones of voice. One may keep in mind events of history, both ancient and modern, but be unable to recite biographical details.

These illustrations show that there is no unitary 'faculty' of memory. 'The "faculty" of memory,' writes Dr A. A. Roback, a modern psychologist, 'would denote that somewhere in the mind there is a force or power which enables us to remember, no matter what the material, whether figures, objects, meaningless words, or significant ideas.'

Questioning whether an understanding of the mind can be based on the view that it is composed of faculties, Dr Roback concludes: 'The chief argument against faculty psychology was that it explained nothing; that it was, therefore, a sterile attempt to give information which was of no value.'[4]

Different Types of Memory

There are two main types of remembering activity. The first is that involved in such apparently simple tasks as writing and speaking, which it would be impossible to carry out unless we had learned and remembered them in childhood. On the other hand, there is the remembering activity involved in attending to a present experience which is determined by a particular past experience, as, for example, when we remember now where we spent our last summer holidays.

The first type of memory is called *habit memory*; the second type is called *pure memory*. When we speak of memory we may mean either or both of these types, although we generally mean the second. In this book we shall be chiefly concerned with pure memory.

Habit memory is the knowledge acquired by experience as distinct from the particular experience of acquiring it. When we have learned to play a piece of music, we are said to remember it, but we may not remember the particular experiences of learning it. Playing a musical composition, which is remembered in the sense of being learned by heart, has all the marks of a habit. Like a habit it is acquired by repetition.

Pure memory, on the other hand, is the activity of attending to a particular experience, as, for example, when I remember what I ate for my Christmas dinner last year.

The past, then, survives under two distinct forms: first, in motor mechanisms (habit); secondly, in independent recollections (pure memory).

Remembering activities are also capable of being classified in various other ways. For instance, there are *immediate memory* and *remote memory*.

When we attempt to reproduce what we have learned, we can do so at once, in which case we are testing immediate memory. For example, when you use the index of a book, you need to remember the page number only long enough to find the reference you want.

One of the simplest memory experiments measures the immediate memory span. A set of letters or a row of numbers in presented, and you are required to reproduce as many as you can remember after seeing or hearing them once only. For example, look at the set of letters on the left below:

```
P    X    M
S    C    L          729438651
Z    N    G
```

Now close the book and try to write down what you saw. Afterwards do the same with the row of numbers.

Few people are able to reproduce more than seven or eight letters or digits correctly. The average immediate memory span for digits is about seven.

Immediate memory is contrasted with remote memory. This is tested when we try to recall something after a lapse of time. If after we have learned a certain lesson we reproduce what we have learned before we have had time to forget any appreciable amount, we speak of immediate memory. If we delay the occasion on which we reproduce the learned material until some time after having learned it, we can then use remote memory.

In addition, memory can be classified on the basis of the method used in memorizing. When we memorize by repetition alone, we are using *rote memory*. On the other hand, when we try to fit the parts into a unified whole, we employ *logical memory*. Usually fewer repetitions are necesary for fixing the facts in mind when the logical method is employed.

The child who learns the multiplication tables is said to employ rote memory, while the adult who learns by observing relationships is said to employ logical memory. Children later begin to learn by logical memorizing, but even the adult does not scorn rote memory at times. This is because the material that he has to learn is not always full of meaning. Such material can, however, often be remembered quite well, especially if a person is interested in it. When we are dealing with material which cannot easily be organized into a meaningful whole, this is where rote memory, which depends purely and simply upon repetition, comes in handy.

For instance, when we are learning words in a foreign language, the form of the word may not have much meaning for us. It may seem to be just a peculiar jumble of syllables that we cannot readily associate with either the English equivalent or any other English word. It is then that we must rely upon rote memory.

Types of Memory Images

Most memory images are inferior in realism to actual sensory experience. That is to say, remembering something is never as vivid as seeing it. But individuals differ greatly in the realism of their memory images.

For example, some children under fourteen, if they examine any picture closely for a few moments and then look at a plain grey background, can see the object as if it were present. They can answer questions about it which they did not have in mind while looking at it. This type of image is called an *eidetic image*. Eidetic imagery seems to fade out during adolescence. Although a few adults can still obtain eidetic images, most are incapable of doing so.

Another type of memory experience which shows considerable individual differences is the *hallucination*. An hallucination is a memory image which seems real, until you awaken to the reality of your surroundings, or because you have lost contact with the objective situation, e.g. in dreams, mental illness. It is built up out of past experience and taken for a present objective fact.

When we see 'something that isn't there,' the hallucination is fabricated out of something already in our mind. Something cannot be created out of nothing in the mental realm any more than it can in the physical realm.

For example, on entering a psychoanalyst's consulting-room a patient thought that he saw a pool of blood in a corner and that the analyst had been murdered by the previous patient. In the course of the analytic session it turned out that it was the patient himself who felt murderous towards the analyst. In projecting the memories of his murderous wishes on to the previous patient, he became convinced that the latter had murdered the analyst.[5]

This incident illustrates how the projection of a memory image leads to the development of an hallucination. The patient 'saw' the blood which wasn't there because he had a reason for doing so. The hallucination was created out of memories that already existed in his own mind.

Such experiences can be produced in the psychological laboratory. One psychologist sat his subjects in a chair, on the arm of which was a small light-bulb. He then sounded a thousand-cycle tone, and at the same time the bulb was lit up. The tone and the light were paired for sixty trials. Eventually thirty-two of forty subjects reported hearing the tone when the light was presented alone.

Four other psychologists were run through the procedure. Two of them were conditioned into hearing the tone as an auditory hallucination. [6]

There are also differences from one person to another regarding the type of imagery they employ in remembering. This naturally leads to distinctive preferences for material presented in a certain way.

For example, the following report illustrates a preference for 'learning by doing': 'I understand by being shown how to do a job and having it explained as I progress, but I am never able to understand much how to do a job by reading about it in a book and following diagrams, etc.'

This person evidently remembers best by means of images of the muscular movements made in carrying out a piece of work. There are also memory images of the senses of sight, hearing, touch, taste and smell.

Many people are visiles, that is to say, they remember better by creating visual images of what they learn. A preference for a visual presentation is revealed in the following report: 'I have to draw a diagram to illustrate the process of thought before I have got it permanently. Otherwise I waste hours memorizing the results.'

This lady's report may be contrasted with the one given above. Another point worth noting is that she is using the word 'memorizing' in a restricted sense. She refers to memorizing verbal materials, such as the words printed in a book. When she draws a diagram, however, she is also memorizing. She is making use of visual memory; that is to say, she finds it more convenient to learn pictorial than verbal material.

On the other hand, another person said that he found it easier to concentrate on material treated orally, i.e. talks or lectures. Such a person is of an imagery type known as an audile. This type can remember better by hearing words than by seeing the printed word.

A few people are tactiles; that is, they can remember things better when they have felt them. Their remembering is based on images of touch. For example, a woman said: 'My memory of touch is far stronger than that of sight. For example, in my mind I can feel a dog's coat, put on its collar, feel it pull at the lead and jump up, sense the warmth of its pads. Or again, I can imagine the vibration of a mechanical digger. But if, for example, I try to remember whether the dog is black or brown, the visual image is vague and soon fades out.'

Here is an interesting example of an olfactory memory, i.e., one based on images of the sense of smell. 'It is quite surprising how many forgotten things come back to mind,' said Mrs H. W. 'Even the smell associated with events of long ago is as real as if I were actually smelling it now.'

Individual differences of this kind exist from person to person, and an attempt has been made to classify individuals into types according to the kinds of images which control their remembering. It has been found, however, that in the great majority of cases this classification does not work out very well in practice. It is doubtful whether a particular person belongs to any one of the above types exclusively, for the majority of people employ both visual and auditory images.

In the words of one psychologist, 'Instead of a few types, there is one type.' This means that most people belong to a mixed type. That is to say, they remember in several different ways, although perhaps one way may predominate, as in the instances cited above.

Hence, it is really up to each person to find the right sort of conditions under which he can memorize most effectively. He may find that it suits him better to say something over aloud a few times to himself, while another person will find it easier to remember by creating a picture in his mind's eye.

Problems with Imagery

'You will no doubt,' writes Alan Baddeley, 'have come across invitations to improve your memory either in the small advertisement section of magazines or perhaps on station bookstands. Such memory training courses involve a number of techniques, but visual imagery almost invariably plays an important role.'[7]

For some people, however, it doesn't. In fact, where imagery is concerned, individuals fall into three broad categories:

1. Those who have no difficulty in forming mental images.
2. Those who have mental images but with varying degrees of difficulty.
3. Those who do not have mental images at all.

Let us examine each group in turn.

1. Mental images with ease. Those who fall in this group will find that applying memory-training methods which call for visualization is no problem at all.

2. Mental images with difficulty. For example, Mr D. P. said: 'I am troubled by my apparent inability to form mental pictures of people. If I think of an ark, I cannot picture Noah. If I think of the law, I cannot visualize a policeman. I can't even picture myself without staring at a picture of myself for some time.' Apart from restricting one's images to animals or inanimate objects, what else can Mr D. P. and others with a similar difficulty do?

Persons in this group can derive encouragement from two sources. One is the fact that mental imagery doesn't have to be all that vivid to be effective as a memory aid. Sir Frederick Bartlett compared people in respect of how well they recalled stories. He found that those who had vivid mental imagery recalled them no more accurately than those who didn't. The difference between the two groups was simply that those who had vivid mental imagery recalled the stories with greater confidence. [8,9]

Secondly, we must draw a distinction between seeing something in the 'mind's eye' and thinking about it. Either is successful as a memory technique. In psychological terms the two abilities are called visual memory and verbal memory. Bartlett found that the subjects who took part in his experiments fell into two categories: visualizers, who remembered by seeing with the mind's eye, and verbalizers, who relied on thinking with words instead of mental pictures.

'People vary enormously,' admits Baddeley, 'in the extent to which they claim to have visual imagery. This is very rarely, if at all, reflected in what they actually recall.' [10] He reminds us, as Bartlett pointed out, that, while visualizers are much more confident about their memory, both groups remember equally well. He suggests a reason for this lack of difference by drawing the now familiar analogy between memory and a computer. He says that mental imagery is like displaying the stored information on a TV screen, while thinking is like displaying it on a print-out, but in either case the output is the same. [11]

'What is recalled,' he adds, 'is determined by what is stored, not by the preferred method of display. The visual imagers may be using an equivalent of a cathode ray tube and the verbalizers the equivalent of a teleprinter, but since both draw on a single abstract store, the accuracy of what they recall will not differ.' [12]

Potter and Faulconer conducted an experiment in which they gave their subjects the names of various categories. The subjects were then shown either a picture of an item or its name and were asked to say whether the item belonged to the category in question. The experimenters found that both tasks were done rapidly, pictures being classified somewhat faster than words. They concluded that their experiment 'supports the hypothesis of a single abstract memory system which contains both linguistic and pictorial information and which can be accessed equally well by words or pictures.' [13]

3. *No mental images.* 'I do not seem able,' said Mr C. M., 'to conjure up any pictures in my mind's eye. All I get is a blank somewhat like a TV screen when the set is switched off.'

As we have seen, recent research shows that, whether you cannot make mental images clearly or whether you cannot make them at all, this need not prejudice your chances of improving your memory.

If you cannot make mental images at all, there are two things that you can do. One has already been described. It is that you can rely on verbal memory or thinking. For example, Miss M. B. said: 'I have taken mind-development courses in the past, but I always come up against the same difficulty: inability to visualize despite months of practice. How can I learn it? I do not appear to have mental images corresponding to any of the five senses. Instead of visualizing pictures I invariably "see" the printed word.' This implies that, say, people have to be remembered not by their faces but by descriptions of their faces.

But there are other types of memory besides visual and verbal memory, and you may also be able to rely on one or more of these. They are based upon information derived through the senses. Memory aids which make use of visual imagery employ the sense of sight. But there are also images based on hearing (auditory), touch (tactile), and smell (olfactory). Some people even have taste imagery (gustatory).

A student said that, although he had the greatest difficulty in forming visual images, he could easily recall the sounds of music, humming bees, running water, whistling wind, rustling leaves. This is auditory memory.

In his short story *Young Goodman Brown* Nathaniel Hawthorne describes a forest in terms of auditory imagery. 'The whole forest,' he writes, 'was peopled with frightful sounds — the creaking of the trees, the howling of wild beasts, and the yell of Indians; while sometimes the wind tolled like a distant church-bell, and sometimes gave a broad roar around the traveller, as if all Nature were laughing him to scorn.'

Mr E.S. said: 'I recalled being comforted by my father when I could have been only three or four years of age. I could remember the feel of the coarse material of his waistcoat on my face.' This is a tactile memory image.

Miss H. B. D. said: 'I have always had a very good memory. When I was two years old, I managed to escape from the house and get run over. I was crushed all down one side, and my left arm was torn from the socket. Although I don't remember the pain, I can still hear my shrieks while a doctor was attending me. When I was a young girl, we went to live in Montreal for three years. In the autumn there were sensations which will live in my memory for ever. I still smell the sharp tang of the grapes which seemed to grow everywhere, and hear the noise of the bullfrogs that sang all night on the banks of the St. Lawrence.' Miss H. B. D. can 'smell with the mind's nose' ('I still smell the sharp tang of the grapes'). She can 'hear with the mind's ear' ('I can still hear my shrieks . . . and the noise of the bullfrogs that sang all night').

Ways of Remembering

Remembering, as we see, is not a simple but a complex act. A study of the process permits us to distinguish three separate aspects. In other words, when we remember there are three ways in which we do so.

We can study something to commit it to memory. For example, we can repeat a poem to learn it by heart. This is called *memorizing*.

Secondly, we can try to bring to mind something we have temporarily forgotten. For example, we memorized a friend's telephone number yesterday and today we try to think what it was. When the attempt is successful, this memory activity is known as *recalling*.

Sometimes events are recalled differently from how they actually happened. They are reconstructed in a way which strikes a person as reasonable and which fits in with his established habits of thought and feeling. There are unintentional inaccuracies in the recall of past experiences. Investigators who have studied this phenomenon of retrospective falsification, as it is called, have reported the existence of tendencies to simplify, generalize, and distort events so that they provide a meaningful and connected narrative.

An example of this occurs in Nevil Shute's *A Town Like Alice*. After the women prisoners believe that Sergeant Joe Harman has been crucified by his Japanese captors for stealing chickens on their behalf, they begin to confuse him with Christ. They did this because most of them had been church-goers and, as Shute puts it, 'deep in their hearts they had been longing for the help of God.' He continues: 'As the weeks went on, accurate memory of the Australian began to fade, and was replaced by an awed and roseate memory of the man he had not been.'

We have seen what must happen to an item between memorizing it and recalling it. Obviously, it must somehow be recorded in the brain, otherwise we should be unable to recall it at all. The image was impressed on the mind and some trace of the impression remains. If nothing of it remained, nothing could be revived. The memory activity which keeps, say, the date of the Battle of Hastings in our heads, even though we are not consciously thinking of it, is called *retaining* or *retention*.

There are, then, three ways in which we remember. We memorize, we retain and we recall. Memory depends upon (1) the acquirement of the idea or image to be recalled; (2) the ability to retain the impression which has been made; and (3) the ability to revive or recognize the impression which has been retained. Remembering is to be reduced essentially to these three functions.

The practical question with everyone who would strengthen his memory and make it serviceable and reliable is how to get an idea into the mind so as to get it out again on demand. From a practical point of view the most important of the three functions are the first and third: the acquirement of an idea or image and the recall of that idea or image to consciousness. This furnishes the key to a scientific training of the memory.

Memory and Intelligence
What is the relation, if any, between memory and intelligence? Does

a good memory imply that its possessor has a high IQ? Does a poor memory go with low intelligence?

Intelligence, like the control unit in a computer, is an overall function that governs all three stages of memory: input (learning), processing (retention), and output (recall). Between it and memory, however, there is no one-to-one relation. We cannot say that the more intelligent a person is, the better his memory is bound to be. It is a matter of common observation that the brainiest people can sometimes be the most forgetful. The absent-minded professor has become a stock character or stereotype illustrating this point.

Equally, we cannot claim that the less intelligent a person is, the worse his memory is likely to be. This is disproved by the existence of people of low intelligence who have a highly-developed memory. The *idiot savant* has phenomenal recall for one particular kind of material that absorbs his total interest.

There are on record a number of such geniuses. Some of the most outstanding belong to the eighteenth and nineteenth centuries. For example, the untaught English arithmetician Jedediah Buxton (1705-74) possessed singular powers of calculation and a remarkable faculty for solving the most difficult problems. On a visit to London he was taken to see Garrick in *Richard III* and employed himself in counting the words used by the actors. He calculated the product of a farthing doubled one hundred and thirty-nine times. This result, expressed in pounds, runs to thirty-nine figures. He then multiplied this number by itself. He was introduced to the Royal Society, before which he gave some demonstrations of his calculating powers. Although Jedediah Buxton's father was a schoolmaster, he himself never learned to write and was employed all his life as a farm labourer. Apart from his calculating genius his intellect was less than mediocre. His inability to acquire the rudiments of education seems to have been caused by his absorbing passion for mathematical calculations, which occupied his mind to the exclusion of all else.

What, then, is the relation between memory and intelligence? We can probably answer this question by saying that the more intelligent you are, the more adequate your associations will be. Given this, the better you are likely to remember. On the other hand, a high level of intelligence does not necessarily mean that you are keenly interested in or attentive to what you wish to remember. Absence of these qualities will tend to hamper your memory. You may have a modest intelligence but a high interest in the subject you are studying. For this reason you may remember it better than someone of superior intelligence whose interest is lacking. You may also, regardless of your level of intelligence, be a persistent kind of person. If either interest or persistence leads you to work hard at what you wish to remember, this, too, will help to guarantee your remembering it.

Another variable that intervenes between intelligence and memory is age. A study by Gilbert has a bearing upon this point. Gilbert gave eleven different memory tests to 174 subjects aged 20 to 29 and to another 174 subjects between 60 and 69 years of age. He found that the older subjects were inferior to the younger ones in all the tests, but that the more intelligent elderly subjects evidenced less deterioration than the less intelligent ones. [14]

It is popularly believed that the ability to remember diminishes with age. However, the amount of deterioration depends on the nature of the material. Gilbert concluded that elderly subjects evince relatively little decline in immediate memory for simple material, but that they suffer rather more in their ability to remember the new and unfamiliar.

Other studies show that there is also a decline in intelligence in old age, although this, too, like memory, is subject to qualification. The general conclusion to be drawn is that the amount of decline of intelligence in old age depends upon the initial level of the subject's IQ. Miles and Miles found, for instance, that, at the age of eighty, the individual whose IQ was 130 in early adulthood still has an IQ of 115 or more. The person whose IQ was a normal 100 in early adulthood still has an IQ of 115 or more. The person whose IQ was a normal 100 in earlier years has dropped to 85. The one who was low normal in early adulthood has dropped to a subnormal level by the age of eighty. [15,16,17]

The above studies consider memory in the sense of recall. If it is considered in the sense of memorizing or learning, studies almost invariably show poorer learning by the mentally retarded. [18,19]

Benefits of a Good Memory

When we say that a person has a good memory, we mean that he is able to remember readily what he wishes to remember. In other words, his memory is both retentive and selective. A so-called 'photographic' memory, on the other hand, is actually a disadvantage because it means that the mind is cluttered up with inessential details that there is no need to remember.

The Russian psychologist Luria studied a memory expert known as S., who experienced the embarrassment of being unable to forget what he did not wish to remember. He could not exercise the creative process of selecting those elements of experience which produce a meaningful pattern of memory. Without such selectiveness our mental life would be chaotic in the extreme. Although most of us would like to be able to remember more than we do, it would be intolerable if we could never forget anything at all. This book aims at assisting the reader to achieve the former state, not the latter.

The case of S. shows that a perfect memory can be a mixed blessing. But this is not to deny the undoubted advantages of a good reliable memory. Its benefits can readily be seen to rank highly in everyday affairs, sometimes in obvious ways, sometimes in less obvious ones.

For example, you can use your memory to win friends and influence people. In *The King and His Court* Pierre Viansson-Ponte says that, if the late President de Gaulle wished to charm, he employed his phenomenal memory. He records an incident when a financier called to discuss an intricate problem which involved eleven points. After he had recited all the points, the President took up each one in order and gave his advice on them all in turn. 'The financier,' remarks the author, 'left stupefied with admiration and permanently won over.'

'Learning how to concentrate and memorize,' said Mr I. H. K., 'has enhanced my social position. It's a real brain booster!'

A good memory can make the difference between getting and losing a job. A man went for an interview for a job at a power-station. As both he and the interviewer were ex-soldiers, the interviewer asked him what was the weight of an army rifle. He could not remember. 'I made such a mess of this and other questions,' he admitted, 'that I knew I had lost the job.' 'I question men on their military careers,' said the interviewer. 'It helps me in trying to make a correct assessment of potential.'

Once a job is secured, memory comes into its own in performing its duties. Without a good memory, you can't do them properly, whatever they are. For example, Mr B. P. said: 'I am a stand-up comic who can't remember his jokes. It's no laughing matter coming off stage after only five or ten minutes when you're supposed to do twenty! A fear of forgetting comes over me when I get in front of the audience.'

How a faulty memory led to the loss of a job is seen in the case of a Lancashire parson. According to the Press, he started a communion service having forgotten to provide the bread. He forgot to attend weddings at the right times. His parochial church council complained to their bishop, and the bishop's interview with the vicar led to the latter's resignation. A member of the council described him as 'terribly absent-minded'. The vicar admitted: 'I have been under a lot of strain recently.'

A good memory can favour your academic success. For example, a Lincolnshire schoolboy, who took his 11-plus at nine, gained 1st-class passes in seven GCE 'O' Level subjects at fourteen, three 'A' Levels with honours at fifteen, and won a scholarship to St. Peter's College, Oxford, at sixteen. 'When I want a fact,' he said, 'I just close my eyes and imagine a textbook or a blackboard I have seen, then read the answer.' This young man's father also had a retentive memory. 'If someone reads a poem to me,' he said, 'I can recite it almost word for word.'

The above are some obvious ways which point up the value of a sound memory. Less obvious ways include saving money, saving life, combating crime, and overcoming boredom.

For example, memory can save you money. A man was taking £400 to the bank in a paper bag. While he opened the door of his garage, he put the bag on the boot of his car. He drove away forgetting about the money, which fell off and was lost.

When a person has an accident, he often forgets the events that immediately preceded it. For example, a holiday-maker fell out of a third-floor bedroom window of an hotel in Ibiza, sustaining multiple injuries, which included a fractured skull. When he recovered consciousness, he was unable to recall anything about the holiday other than arriving at the resort. Questioning and coaxing by his family at his hospital bedside failed to elicit the forgotten memories. The memory loss persisted in spite of improvement in the victim's physical condition. This case underlines the importance of a good memory from a financial point of view. Although covered by insurance, the holiday-maker could claim compensation only by remembering how the fall occurred.

Again, somebody's ability to remember could save your life. A young man read an article on mouth-to-mouth resuscitation. Later he was to save the life of a child who fell into a pond. Brought out unconscious, the child was revived by the young man's application of what he remembered from the article.

A good memory can combat crime. A shop manageress's memory for faces led to the arrest and conviction of a gang of two men and three women who are professional shop-lifters. She spotted them in the city centre of Wakefield, W. Yorks., remembered their having acted suspiciously in her own shop six months previously, and tipped off the police. Detectives followed the gang into a clothes shop and caught them red-handed. At Wakefield City Court they were each given a six-month suspended gaol sentence.

Another advantage of memory is that it can be used as a means of overcoming boredom. Faced with the need to kill time while in prison, Meursault, the hero of Albert Camus's *The Outsider*, applies this technique.

'Once I'd learnt the trick of remembering things,' we read, 'I never had a moment's boredom. Sometimes I would exercise my memory on my bedroom, and, starting from a corner, make the round, noting every object I saw on the way. At first it was over in a minute or two. But each time I repeated the experience, it took a little longer. I made a point of visualizing every piece of furniture, and each article upon or in it, and then every detail of each article, and finally the details of the details, so to speak: a tiny dent or incrustation, or a chipped edge, and the exact grain and colour of the woodwork . . . I found that the more I thought, the more details, half-forgotten or malobserved, floated up from my memory. There seemed no end to them.

'So I learned that even after a single day's experience of the outside world a man could easily live a hundred years in prison. He'd have laid up enough memories never to be bored.'

Perhaps with a novelist's licence Camus exaggerates slightly in his final statement, but the general idea that he has lighted upon is sound enough.

2.

Why We Forget

We have seen that the things we experience form mental pictures which are impressed on our brain as memory traces. Each trace is accompanied by a certain amount of mental energy, which is drawn from other memory traces already laid down. The reason for this is that a person has just so much mental energy to invest in the experiences he undergoes.

When a memory trace had little energy to begin with or has lost it to other memory traces, the experience it represents is said to be forgotten. The trace may not be charged with much initial energy because the experience did not make much of an impression in the first place. On the other hand, the energy it had originally may have been drained off in the formation of new memory traces. The learning of something new usually means that something old has to be unlearned.

A trace which has lost its energy can be recharged by repeating the experience which originally laid it down. This is known as refreshing one's memory. For example, when one forgets a telephone number one can recharge the memory trace by looking the number up in the telephone book.

A poor memory is caused, then, by the memory trace not having much energy to begin with, by not being recharged or fading with the lapse of time, and by losing its energy to other memory traces. That is to say, the causes of forgetting may be grouped under the following headings:

1. Weak impression.
2. Disuse.
3. Interference.

There is also a form of forgetting, known as repression, caused by resistance or opposition from something else in the mind to the recall of the desired memory. We may, therefore, add the following heading:

4.   Repression.

Let us consider each of these headings in further detail.

1.   Weak Impression
The first cause of forgetting is not properly attending to what we wish to remember. The result is that the experience does not make a strong enough impression on us.

Attention means directing mental activity towards a mental or physical object or situation. For example, when I think of something I did last week, I am attending to my memory of the event. This memory is a mental object. On the other hand, when I admire a beautiful view, I am attending to a physical object.

Attention is to the mind what the power of focusing the lens is to a camera. If the camera is not properly focused, the resulting photograph will not be clear. So a wobbly, vagrant mind does not get clear pictures and consequently finds it difficult to bring them back to memory.

Upon the clearness and truth of first impressions must depend the ease and speed of their reproduction. We cannot hope to recall past events or experiences with certainty if our perception of them is not clear and reliable.

A young man said: 'I have a poor memory for names of people, books and places. This failing is worse when I am in the company of important and influential people.'

This problem illustrates the effect of inattention upon memory. When he is in the company of influential people, he is probably thinking of the impression which he is making upon them. When their names are announced or when some book or place is mentioned, he probably does not remember it because he is not really attending to it.

The law of attention is that we cannot attend to two separate things at the same time. For example, we cannot simultaneously entertain two opposite thoughts, like 'I am a success' and 'I am a failure'. This law is called by Dr Henry Knight Miller in his book *Practical Psychology* the law of predominant mental impression. [20]

Although many people try to attend to more than one thing at once, they succeed only in alternating their attention. The attention of the person who is apparently capable of, say, reading a book while he listens to the radio really shifts backwards and forwards in quick succession from one to the other.

The practical use of the law of attention is seen when we realize that it is the first step in all the higher mental processes. The art of memory is primarily the art of attention. We forget because we do not pay sufficient attention to what we wish to remember in order to imprint it firmly on the mind. A good memory, therefore, depends upon attention to what is to be remembered. Since one cannot attend to more than one thing at once, *give your full attention to what you wish to remember*.

2. Disuse

The second cause of a faulty memory is letting the trace fall into disuse, or not repeating the experience in order to refresh the memory.

It is normal to forget most of what is learned within a few days after learning it — unless it is constantly revised to keep it fresh in mind. For example, a man said: 'Whenever I read a book I grasp with ease what it contains, but unfortunately after only a few days I forget almost all of it. What can I do about this?'

A memory trace tends to decay with the lapse of time. For example, another man admitted: 'I have a shocking memory. Whatever I study in the morning is forgotten by evening.'

Much of what we learn is forgotten almost as soon as we have learned it. The little that remains after that is forgotten more slowly. The psychologist Ebbinghaus, who carried out the most important early work on memory, found that after one hour 56 per cent of the material which he had studied was forgotten; but after nine hours only a further 8 per cent had been forgotten; after two days only a further 6 per cent, and only a further 7 per cent after as long as one month. In other words, about 70 per cent of the amount which was forgotten in the first month was forgotten in the first hour of that month. Consequently, it is most economical to refresh our memory about something as soon as possible afterwards, rather than to wait until some time has elapsed. [21]

This principle is important not only in learning but in teaching, especially in such forms of 'teaching' as propaganda, direct-mail advertising, etc. In other words, if a person reads a sales letter, he will give it his best attention at the time but in spite of this he is likely to forget most of it quite soon afterwards. The rate of forgetting, which is rapid in the first few hours, becomes less rapid later on.

Therefore, how are we to plan a direct-mail advertising campaign in which we are sending out to potential customers a series of, say, six letters about our product? Are we to send one a week for six weeks, or ought we to bunch them together at the start? The above principle suggests that the second method would be the more effective, because if further letters follow immediately after the first one they will have the effect of reinforcing it before the potential customer has forgotten too much of its message.

Although Ebbinghaus worked with nonsense syllables, the same general principle also applies to relatively meaningful material, like follow-up letters, except that meaningful material is as a rule better retained in the memory than meaningless material. It is still true, however, that the rate at which meaningful material is forgotten is also most rapid immediately after it has been studied and less rapid later on.

Experimenting with the same problem, psychologist A. R. Gilliland of Northwestern University found a slower falling off in the rate of initial forgetting in the case of pictures. He showed his subjects pictures, about which he later asked them questions. They were tested immediately after seeing the pictures, and two days, seven days, and thirty days later. One group after two days recalled over four-fifths of what they recalled immediately after seeing the pictures. This points to the effectiveness of suitably chosen visual material in learning, teaching, presenting a sales message, and so on. [22]

A second follow-up reminder is more effective if it is sent out very soon after the first one, but unless it is sent then, it does not matter much whether it is sent ten or thirty days later. The reason is that far more of the message will be forgotten in the first day after the letter is read than between the second and thirtieth days after. The receipt of the second letter should arrest the process of forgetting which began immediately after the prospect had read the first. It refreshes his memory before he has forgotten too much.

That advertisers are aware of the importance of following up soon afterwards may readily be noticed in the course of an evening's TV viewing. It is not at all uncommon to see that the same product is advertised two or three times in the course of the same evening. It is designed to ensure maximum impact for the advertiser's message.

3. Interference

The above view, however, is too simple. It is now known that other activities we pursue after learning something interfere with our ability to remember it. Forgetting is due not so much to the passage of time but rather to what happens during the passage of time — to interference occurring between one set of memories and another. This is of two kinds.

We have seen that the material which is newly learned forms a memory trace somewhere in the brain. This is like a plastic material which takes some time to set or consolidate, after which it becomes a part of our store of memories.

However, during the process of hardening or consolidation the memory trace is still susceptible to interference from other mental activities. What happens now interferes with what has happened in the past. Psychologists call this 'retroactive inhibition'. We forget something because of what we do and think afterwards.

'I can wake in the night,' said Mr R. E., 'and go over a dream methodically from beginning to end, trying to memorize it. But in the morning it escapes me. I don't know why.'

This is an example of retroactive inhibition. It is likely that after he had gone to sleep again, he had further dreams. These caused him to forget the dream which he had committed to memory during the period of wakefulness.

In terms of study, retroactive inhibition means that we forget something we have learned because we have learned other things subsequently. The amount of forgetting depends on the similarity of the material learned now to the material learned in the past. Interference is most active when the interfering material is most similar to the material originally learned.

An experiment compared four groups of subjects. All of them learned a list of adjectives. Then one group learned other adjectives. Another learned unrelated material such as 3-digit numbers or nonsense syllables. A third group read a selection of jokes. And the fourth group simply rested. When the four groups were retested on the original list of adjectives, the subjects who had rested forgot less than those who learned unrelated material. Forgetting was greater when other adjectives were learned during the interval and greatest of all when the later adjectives were synonyms of those in the first list. The group that had learned synonyms remembered only 12 per cent of the original list as compared with 37 per cent remembered by the group that had learned numbers and 45 per cent by the group that had read jokes. The experiment clearly demonstrates the adverse effect of learning material similar to the material originally learned.[23]

In Sir Arthur Conan Doyle's story *The Hound of the Baskervilles* the effect of retroactive inhibition is described in the words of Sherlock Holmes. Dr Watson asks Holmes to give him a sketch of the course of events from memory. Holmes replies that he cannot guarantee to carry all the facts in his mind, adding that intense mental concentration has a way of blotting out what has passed.

'The barrister,' he continues, 'who has his case at his fingers' end, and is able to argue with an expert upon his own subject, finds that a week or two of the courts will drive it all out of his head once more. So each of my cases displaces the last.'

Dave Browne, the hero of Brian Rothery's novel *The Storm*, reflecting on his past, thinks of certain incidents as part of a story rather than 'real memories that pulled at every fibre in his being'. He attributes this to the passing of time, but the author makes him go on to ask: 'What was the loss process like?' He describes the influence of retroactive inhibition in the following terms:

> As it was hardly likely that the stored pictures simply shed their values over time, it must be that the same memory locations that stored these pictures were used also to house pictures from new experiences, which meant that new pictures crowded out the old, not pushing them out completely, but allowing only a mere skeleton code to remain.

There is a second way in which interference occurs. This is when what has happened previously interferes with what is happening now. Work which *precedes* learning also tends to interfere with the retention of the learned material. What happened before an experience causes us to forget it as well as what happened afterwards. This is known as 'proactive inhibition'. For example, a secretary wanted to know whether, having learned Pitman 2000 shorthand seven years earlier (but forgotten it), she could now learn Pitman New Era shorthand. An affirmative answer to the question is possible, but having learned Pitman 2000 will both help and hinder her in learning New Era. Doubtless between 2000 and New Era there are certain similarities in the general principles involved. The fact that she has already familiarized herself with these by learning 2000 (even though she claims to have forgotten it) will make it easier for her to learn whatever parts of New Era employ the same general principles. On the other hand, if we apply proactive inhibition to her case, it means that her previous learning of 2000 will tend to interfere with her recall of the new material which she learns from New Era.

A classic example of this interference is the case of the late Professor A. C. Aitken of the University of Edinburgh. He was a mathematician with a remarkable memory who learned the value of *pi* to 1,000 decimal places. Twenty-one years later he discovered, somewhat to his chagrin, that he had to relearn 180 of the digits because they had been incorrect in the first place. This proved a bit troublesome because the 180 incorrect digits which he had previously memorized interfered with the learning of the new ones.

'It so often happens,' said Mr C. L., 'that when I set out to do two things, after I have done the first I forget the second. For example, I may go to the shop to buy 250g of butter and some envelopes. I may buy the butter and forget the envelopes. Another example is: I tender a coin or note for bus fare; the conductor tells me: "No change. I'll give it to you later". At the end of the journey I forget to ask for it and the conductor "conveniently" forgets too.'

Both experiences illustrate proactive inhibition.

Again, our inability to remember the content of a chapter from a history textbook may be determined by the fact that beforehand we had done some reading in sociology.

All this illustrates that forgetting is a process of mutual interference or inhibition among the various items of information that have accumulated in our minds as a result of our reading.

Proactive inhibition affects remembering on three levels. It prevents us from memorizing properly; it prevents us from retaining properly, and it also prevents us from recalling properly.

One of the commonest sources of proactive inhibition is emotional in nature. Interference by inner emotional conflicts is apt to be a prime cause of forgetting the material we read. It affects our capacity to register what we see on the printed page. Not registering it properly, we are unable to recall it properly. 'Emotion', said Dr Janet, 'makes people absent-minded.'

As we saw in the first chapter, in learning something new there is unlearning of something old. The story is told of a man who was an authority on fish. He liked to be able to call everybody he met by name. It is said, however, that every time he learned the name of a person he forgot the name of a fish.

4. Repression

There is also a method of unconscious forgetting of painful memories known as 'repression'. Repression is 'the keeping of unacceptable ideas from consciousness, i.e., in the "unconscious." '[24] It is the unconscious process whereby we prevent ourselves from becoming aware of some tendency active in the mind. It occurs when two forces in the mind are opposed to each other, the desire to recall being countered by a strong resistance or wish not to recall.

For example, when Berlioz, the famous French composer, was poverty-stricken and his wife was ill, there came to him one night the inspiration for a symphony. He rose from bed, beginning to write, but in his own words he thought:

> If I begin this bit, I shall have to write the whole symphony. It will be a big thing, and I shall have to spend three or four months over it. That means I shall write no more articles and earn no more money . . . The poor invalid will lack necessities, and I shall be able to pay neither my personal expenses nor my son's fees when he goes on board ship. These thoughts made me shudder, and I threw down my pen, saying, 'Bah, to-morrow I shall have forgotten the symphony.' But the next night I heard the allegro clearly and seemed to see it written down . . . I was going to get up, but the reflections of the day before restrained me. I steeled myself against the temptation and clung to the thoughts of forgetting it. At last I went to sleep, and the next day upon wakening all remembrance of it had indeed gone for ever.

Berlioz had, in fact, repressed the memory of the symphony.

Freud has compared repression with what might have happened to a book containing objectionable statements at a time when books were written out by hand. The offending passages would be heavily crossed out, so that when the book was transcribed, gaps in the text would make the passages unintelligible. Or words would be replaced by others and whole new sentences interpolated. Without pressing the analogy too closely, we may say that repression of memories is like the corruption of the text of a book.

Why are memories repressed? It is for two reasons. If a person were to become aware of what is repressed, it would make him anxious and upset him. We more easily forget a memory which conflicts with our comfort or self-esteem than one which does not. This is the law of forgetting by repression. For example, a man said: 'Very occasionally I experience a dream. Then it is usually a horrible one and I forget it as fast as I can. Later I cannot recall even the broadest outline of it.' He unconsciously prevented himself from remembering the dream, because the memory made him feel uncomfortable or clashed with his self-esteem.

The second reason is that, although what is repressed may not be unpleasant in itself, it is forgotten because it is associated with something else which is unpleasant. For example, it is easier to forget an appointment to visit the dentist than it is to forget a date to go dancing with a pretty girl. Another instance of unconsciously intentional forgetting due to an experience being associated with something unpleasant is provided by the report of a young man who said: 'When attending dancing lessons I feel so foolish and am always successful in forgetting completely any date made for future private lessons, though usually I do not have a forgetful mind'.

(a) Experimental Proofs of Repression
The occurrence of repression has been demonstrated in the psychological laboratory by means of the following experiment which shows that pleasant experiences are recalled more easily than unpleasant ones.

On returning from the Christmas vacation, a group of college students were asked to record their memories of the vacation. Each memory was then assessed as pleasant or unpleasant. Six weeks later, when the students were retested, the pleasant memories were remembered better than the unpleasant ones. Fifty-three per cent of the pleasant memories were recalled as against only 40 per cent of the unpleasant ones. [25]

A psychologist gave his subjects a list of nouns, to which he asked them to reply with adjectives. Whenever they replied with the name of a colour, they received a mild electric shock. After a while some of them not only stopped naming colours, but apparently failed to think of colours at all. The colour adjectives had been repressed because they had painful associations. [26]

A similar experiment which demonstrates the existence of this mental process is as follows. A list of words was presented to subjects who were asked to give their associations to each one. In the list the word 'red' was followed by the word 'barn' six times, and whenever this occurred the subject received an unexpected electric shock. The experimenter found that the word which had been followed by the electric shock was forgotten by half of his subjects. [27]

Other experimental proofs of forgetting by repression have been reviewed by Blum and by Zeller. [28,29]

According to the psychoanalysts, repression is responsible for maladjustment and emotional ill health. We ought, then, to find that the more a person accepts himself the better adjusted he should be. Conversely, the less a person accepts himself the less well adjusted he should be.

This proposition has been validated by the experimental findings of Taylor and Combs. They compared two similar groups of children. One group was composed of better-adjusted children, as assessed by a personality test; the other group of less well-adjusted children, as assessed by the same test.

The psychologists then compiled a list of twenty statements which they regarded as probably true of all children, yet unflattering if admitted to be true, e.g. 'I sometimes disobey my parents', 'I sometimes tell lies', 'I sometimes steal things when I know I will not be caught'. The list was presented to both groups of children, and each child was asked to check those statements which were true for him.

The results of the experiment corroborated the psychologists' expectation. They demonstrated that the better adjusted a person is, the better he is able to accept damaging statements about himself. The less well adjusted he is, the greater his resistance against accepting such statements. This experiment confirms the psychoanalytical finding about the connection between maladjustment and the repression of unpleasant truths about oneself. [30]

(b) Memory Optimists and Pessimists

Most people, then, remember pleasant experiences better than unpleasant ones. They are known as 'memory optimists'. For example, a woman may remember the pleasure of holding her baby for the first time better than she remembers the pains of childbirth. Thomas Hood wrote:

> I remember, I remember, the house where
> I was born,
> The little window where the sun came
> peeping in each morn.

He remembered his birthplace because he found it pleasant to do so. The poet's childhood days were the happiest that he knew.

Another example is that of Mr I. R., who said: 'I have been unsuccessful in trying to recall the name of a person whom I disliked intensely when I knew him fifteen years ago.'

One might object, however, that after fifteen years the name might have been forgotten even if he had been emotionally neutral to the man or had liked him. This is true. The above experience, in fact, also illustrates another law of memory.

This is the law of recency, which states that the more recent an experience the better it is remembered. Conversely, the less recent an experience the less well it is remembered. The above name was forgotten not only because it was associated with an unpleasant memory, but also because it was fifteen years ago since it was first learned.

This leads to the question: But there are some things which we remember very well even though they happened long ago; why is this? For example, elderly people can often clearly recall events from their childhood, while they may have forgotten what they were doing ten minutes ago.

This is a special case of forgetting due not to psychological causes but to physical ones. These people are undergoing brain changes with age which impair the retention of recent material. The changes do not, however, disturb the more firmly embedded remote memories of childhood.

The fact that not all people remember pleasant experiences better than unpleasant ones is illustrated by the following reports of persons who may be classed 'memory pessimists'. For example, a young man said: 'The memories I recall best are always the same unhappy ones over and over again. I feel that I cannot relax enough to allow my mind to accept any other than these morbid thoughts'.

'When I think back', said a young woman, 'the only things that spring to mind are my failures and moments of embarrassment'.

Another lady, Mrs H. F., reported: 'Generally speaking, I find it less difficult to recall the names of people with whom I have had unhappy associations, even when I have not seen or heard of them for fifteen or twenty years.' Her experience, too, illustrates that an unpleasant emotion may contribute to imprinting a memory on the mind so well that it can be recalled after a considerable lapse of time.

Thompson and Witryol investigated the types of unpleasant experiences which adults recall most frequently. Three groups of fifty adults were asked to recall for twenty minutes unpleasant experiences from three periods of childhood and adolescence. From the first five years of life they recalled more physically unpleasant experiences. From the ages of six to twelve years they recalled more unpleasant experiences related to learning to live in a social world. From the ages of twelve to eighteen they recalled more unpleasant experiences generating feelings of inadequacy and insecurity. [31]

Suppose that a woman were to claim that she remembers the pain of childbirth better than the pleasure of holding her baby for the first time. In such a case we might find that the woman had not really wanted a child at all. Holding the baby in her arms for the first time may have been experienced as unpleasant. It may even have been more unpleasant than the pains of childbirth. The woman, therefore, chose to remember the less unpleasant of the two experiences. The less painful memory was more pleasant to her than the more painful one.

The fact seems to be, however, that emotionally charged experiences, whether pleasant or unpleasant, are remembered better than those experiences which are emotionally neutral. At present this point cannot be definitely established. Yet we may say that if two experiences can be recalled equally well and if one is pleasant and the other unpleasant, most of us would probably prefer to remember the pleasant one.

Therefore, we should try to associate what we learn with something pleasant. For example, the name of an hotel can be remembered by associating it with the pleasant holiday we spent there. If we have difficulty in learning a subject, we can use our imagination to picture what it will mean to us to master the material which we are studying. Then we shall experience a feeling of satisfaction which will help us to remember it better.

The causes of forgetting may now be briefly summarized as follows:

1. We forget an experience because it makes a weak impression on us unless we attend to it properly.
2. We forget an experience because we don't refresh our memory of it.
3. We forget an experience because other experiences interfere with it.
4. We forget an experience because it creates a conflict between the wish to remember it and the wish not to remember it.

(c) Lack of Early Memories (Infantile Amnesia)

Before turning to the practical application of the above principles, we may refer to three special problems which forgetting raises. The first is the problem, which everyone encounters, of what Freud called 'the failure of memory for the first years of our lives'. The second, which we have briefly touched upon in the previous section, is the loss of memory in ageing persons. The third is the feeling that we sometimes get of 'remembering' having seen or done something before when we know that we cannot have seen or done it.

Freud was the first to draw scientific attention to the problem of the lack of memories for the earliest period of our lives. He refers to 'the peculiar amnesia which veils from most people (not from all) the first years of their childhood, usually the first six or eight years'.

Why can't we remember what happened to us in our early infancy? There are several reasons[32]:

(1) *Lack of development of mnemonic capacities.* The areas of the brain involved in conscious memory are not fully developed in early infancy.

(2) *Lack of consciousness of self.* In early infancy we have not yet developed the idea that we are individuals, and consequently we do not remember the events of this period as happening to *us*.

(3) *Inability of the infant to verbalize.* We rely on words with which to form memories, and in early infancy we have not yet learned any words. Most adult thinking is done with words or at least with images of things that have names. Before the age of three a person does not know many words or the names of many things. So all that can come to mind is an unnamed feeling about some unnamed thing. When people have such feelings and don't know where they come from, they may refer to this period preceding the use of words.

(4) *Inability to conceptualize time.* The idea of remembering anything

at all implies the ability to distinguish between past and present. The infant has not yet learned how to do this.

(5) *Repression*. Those experiences of early life that we do retain in the form of fantasies have been repressed from conscious memory because they conflict with the demands of reality. According to the doctrine of infantile amnesia propounded by Freud, the experiences of the first six to eight years are cloaked by a curtain of repression.

We have already encountered all but one of these reasons in our discussion of the causes of forgetting in general. The second, third and fourth reasons all come under the heading of 'weak impression'. The infant's lack of consciousness of self and his inability to use words and conceptualize time mean that his experiences do not impress him strongly enough to be recalled later. The fifth reason, too, applies perhaps more to childhood forgetting than to adult forgetting, since it is in childhood that the basic repressions determining our character are laid down. The first reason is a special physiological one that applies only to childhood.

We see, then, that infantile amnesia is really no more than a special case of the general problem of forgetting. The causes of forgetting in general also account for the particular kind of forgetting that marks the period of infancy.

Nevertheless, the period of infantile amnesia is often interrupted by isolated fragmentary memories. For example, Mr D. B. said: 'Sometimes when I am lying in bed half-way between being awake and asleep my limbs feel short and plump, and the perspective of everything is as if viewed through a wide-angle lens. I always see the same room. One morning I realized that I was feeling as a young baby must in its first twelve months. Could this, in fact, be a memory from my early childhood?'

Such memories are known as 'screen memories'. If these particular ones are recalled from a period in which most of our experiences have been forgotten, it must be that they are recalled for a special reason.

(d) Early Memories

At the age of about sixty, Goethe, in writing an account of his life, recalled a childhood memory of slinging pieces of crockery out of the window into the street, so that they were smashed to pieces. Freud interprets this memory in relation to the fact that a younger brother was born when Goethe was three. The throwing out of the crockery he recognizes as a symbolic act of getting rid of the troublesome intruder. Freud considers that Goethe recalled this memory in order to remind himself that he eventually succeeded in preventing the second son from disturbing Goethe's close relation with his mother, for the younger child died when Goethe was nine. [33]

One school of thought believes that these screen memories of early childhood have survived because they embody in a crystallized form the individual's general attitude or 'style of life'.

For example, Mr N. S. said: 'I recall how in my childhood I was once forced to disclose what had been till then my greatest secret. As an African, I did not get the chance to go to school until I was twelve. I spent most of my time alone as a shepherd boy. As I grew up, I developed an intense curiosity about how everything came into being. "Why was I born?" I kept on asking myself. In my childish and uneducated way I developed the fantasy that I was born so that the sunlight could strike me before it spread to others. This was to be my "secret". One day, when another boy annoyed me, I retaliated by threatening to withhold the sunlight from him. This provoked such laughter that I could not help asking him why he had laughed at me. His reply shattered my illusion and gave me a shock which determined my general attitude to others from that day. I decided that all men are the same and that secrets are useless.'

Another example is that of Miss S. A., who said: 'I seem to remember posing for a photograph at the front window in my mother's arms. When shown this photo as a schoolgirl I announced that I could remember its being taken, but was laughed down. Two of my brothers are in it, my mother is holding one of my bare feet in her hand, and I am about ten months old.'

We would expect this person to have adopted a style of life in which family ties played a strong part. Such was, in fact, the case. She had assumed the role of mother towards a crippled brother with whom she shared a house. She had received an offer of marriage, which she had hesitated to accept because it involved her in a mental conflict over her obligation to support her brother.

A third example is that of a man who recalled his first day at school. 'My mother took me there,' he said, 'and when she left me I felt that she didn't want me and was just trying to get rid of me.' This man's general attitude to life could be summed up in the words: 'I feel unwanted'. In his social and working life he acted on the assumption that others rejected him. Feeling 'odd man out', he created numerous difficulties for himself in his relations with other people.

Consider the following: 'Charging the other kids in the orphanage a marble each to watch me act in little plays I'd written.' What kind of person would we expect to report this as his or her earliest memory? Obviously, someone to whom an audience and acting were important, perhaps someone who would make the stage a career. According to the Press, this is, in fact, the earliest memory of actress Shirley Ann Field.

A man recalled memories of happenings mostly in the chemical laboratory at his secondary school. 'Some hydrogen gas caught fire,' he said. 'I broke some glass apparatus; a fellow student was burned with nitric acid; another chap tasted some chemical material which he thought afterwards might have been phosphorus. What a state he got himself into from the fear of this!' These memories suggest that his interest in chemistry and chemical experiments had played a prominent part in his life. It does not, in fact, surprise us to learn that he was an industrial chemist.

An elderly woman recalled a memory from her seventh birthday when her grandmother gave her a flower and insects from it got on her pinafore, causing her to run back to her granny for help to get rid of them. Why should this particular memory be recalled from among the thousands of experiences which the lady had had in the last sixty or so years? Because it crystallized, as it were, her attitude towards life in general. This was confirmed by the lady herself, who admitted: 'I have always been a mother to others and have been there to solve their troubles.' She recalled the memory because it crystallized the fact that she had been cast in the role of a motherly figure to whom others had appealed for help. Her grandmother's behaviour had perhaps been for her a kind of pattern on which she had modelled her own behaviour.

Another woman recalled that as a child of five she wanted to wear a piece of jewellery belonging to her older sister. She got into a tantrum when her sister insisted on wearing the jewellery and her father threatened to give her a good hiding for being naughty. It would not be surprising to find that jealousy of her sister had played a prominent part in this woman's emotional life. Such, in fact, turned out to be the case. 'You are right,' she said, 'when you say that strong emotions are tied up with my relationship with my sister. I was very jealous of her boy friends.'

Yet another woman recorded three childhood memories as follows:

1. 'I am about a year old. I am in a baby's high chair, being fed from a spoon. A nanny wearing a cloak with red on it is bending over me. I feel frightened because I wonder whether she is a nurse or whether it is blood on her cloak.'
2. 'I am about four and am being dragged by the arm into a room to see my grandmother in her coffin. I am screaming in terror and struggling to escape.'
3. 'I am about six. A nurse is protesting at my presence in the bedroom where my father is lying ill after an operation. I become terrified and ask to leave.'

These memories have a common theme. It is that the young child is frightened by something she doesn't understand. In the first one she doesn't understand whether it is a red cloak or blood. In the second she doesn't understand the mystery of death, and in the third it is the illness and operation which she doesn't understand.

It would not surprise us to find that a person who recalled these memories would be someone who as an adult was still frightened by what she doesn't understand. This is precisely what was found in the present case, because the woman admitted that one of her emotional problems was a fear of the unknown.

'The first thing I remember in life,' said Mr B. C., 'was being wrapped in a blanket and carried to an air-raid shelter. I also remember another incident when I was screaming as my drunken father pulled my mother's hair.'

These incidents have probably been remembered because they crystallized the sense of insecurity and uncertainty acquired by this man as a result of his childhood experiences, which he described as 'so unpleasant'.

These feelings were reflected in the casual attitude which he displayed towards work and marriage and indeed towards life in general. 'I am twenty-four years of age,' he said. 'My problem is: what do I want to do in life? I honestly don't know. The weeks drift by uninterestingly. Since leaving school I have had eighteen different jobs, none of which I was interested in. I got married four months ago and am now losing interest in marriage. I don't seem to attach any importance to my marriage; in fact, I don't seem to care whether I am married or not.'

All these examples show how a memory survives from childhood because in it is embodied a person's general attitude towards life. But this point of view is applicable not only to memories of actual incidents. It applies equally well to memories of fantasies. That is, if a person recalls from childhood an isolated occasion when he imagined something, what he imagined may be significant for the light it throws upon the kind of person he is.

For example, Mr S. O. recalled a fantasy dating from the age of seventeen when he was in domestic service to a titled lady. He imagined himself being punished for ignoring her order not to use the front stairs. Why from his past life did he recall this particular fantasy?

The answer is that the memory of the fantasy survived because it crystallized his attitude towards life. We are entitled to assume that an attitude of defiance of authority figured in his make-up at the age of seventeen.

(e) Disturbance of Memory for Recent Events (Senile Amnesia)

In discussing infantile amnesia we saw that besides the psychological causes of forgetting, the state of the brain was important. Another period of life in which forgetting is affected by the physiological condition of the body is old age.

As the recording process of memory takes place in the brain, anything that affects the brain must affect the memory. For example, a man was involved in a shooting affray and a bullet grazed his skull, knocking him unconscious. When he recovered he could not even remember the girl who was his fiancée.

There are certain changes in the tissues of the body which are associated with advancing years. They tend to appear progressively when middle life has been passed. Individual persons, however, show wide differences in the date of the appearance and rapidity of evolution of such traits.

One of these traits is a tendency to forget what has just been learned, combined with the absence of impairment of childhood memories. People who are getting on in years may forget events which have occurred a few days, hours or even minutes previously, but they may be able to tell a great deal in detail about the distant past and their childhood.

For example, a man of sixty said: 'I find it difficult to remember what I have read, or the details of a transaction, even immediately afterwards, and this leads to errors of all kinds. Yet I can repeat correctly hymns and poems learned in childhood.'

This phenomenon may also be observed in connection with many organic brain disturbances, such as senile dementia, brain lesions and tumours, and chronic alcoholic poisoning. It is called the Korsakoff syndrome.

Very often the memory gaps are filled in by 'memories' invented either spontaneously or when the patients are asked about their past. In the content of these confabulations Korsakoff found a strong preference for deaths and funerals, although often the content concerned everyday routine.

A pronounced disturbance of memory for recent events will mean that the patients become completely disoriented. This leads them to give some year in the last century as the date, to consider themselves young even if they are well advanced in years, or to mistake the identity of persons around them.

(f) Déjà Vu

An unusual and fascinating type of remembering — or forgetting — is the experience known as false recognition or *déjà vu* ('already seen'). It is, says Freud, 'that strange feeling we perceive in certain moments and situations when it seems as if we had already had exactly the same experience, or had previously found ourselves in the same situation. Yet we are never successful in our efforts to recall clearly those former experiences and situations.' [34]

For example, a young man said: 'At my work I'll be doing a certain job and suddenly I feel I have done this particular job in exactly the same way and in exactly the same conditions some time long before, when actually I haven't.'

'Occasionally,' said another young man, 'when at a dance or at work or in other situations I feel that the whole thing has happened to me before and sometimes I can vaguely sense what is going to happen. This lasts for only a few minutes at a time.'

'During the last six months,' added a third person, 'I have been in several situations which I think I have been in before although I know I haven't. For example, I notice a book open at a certain page. I feel that I expected to see it open at that place. I expect my boss to ask me a certain question. This he does and for the next few minutes everything happens as though I have gone through the same experience before. This has happened several times.'

Yet another person described an experience of *déjà vu* as follows: 'Last year a friend of mine spent his holidays abroad and paid a visit to a city he had never read about or heard very much of. As soon as he arrived there he appeared to be quite conversant with his surroundings. He found his way to his hotel without being directed by anyone, without looking at street names. As he put it, "I just kept on walking until I saw an hotel which I 'recognized' as the one where I was to stay." When he went to his room, this again was quite familiar to him; he knew where everything was placed in it and it seemed to him as if he'd been there all his life. I suggested that he had read about it or spent some time in his past in very similar surroundings. He had tried to find an explanation along these lines, but could think of nothing in his experience to warrant any such solution.'

Déjà vu is described by Dickens in one of his novels where he writes: 'Sometimes we get the feeling as if what we say and do has already been said and done a long time ago, and as if we had seen the same faces, objects and conditions in primeval times, as if we could expect what will now be said, and as if we would suddenly remember this.' The quality of familiarity and inability to recall the previous experience thus characterize *déjà vu*.

What is the explanation of this feeling that we have already experienced something before, although we know that this is impossible?

It is sometimes thought that the experience confirms the theory of reincarnation. That is to say, what is now experienced is familiar because it has actually been experienced before — in a previous incarnation. Psychology is unable to accept this explanation, which Freud describes as 'naïvely mystical and unpsychological'.

Those who have read Shaw Desmond's *Reincarnation for Everyman* will recall that a number of cases, including the author's own, are used in it to defend the reincarnation hypothesis.

For example, Shaw Desmond describes in the following words the clear-cut memories that he claims to have of a former life in Rome as a gladiator in the reign of the Emperor Nero:

I remembered the men I had fought. I recalled something of their technique. And, above all, I remembered the great Nero himself — he who for me . . . is more real than almost anyone I have known in this life.

As a child, I heard again the swish of the sling of the Balearic slingers of death and the whine of the stone. Again and again I would practise childishly with my wooden sword as I had once wielded the sword in the arena.

The same author remembers being killed in the arena by his adversary:

The man, Clistris, who did me to death that day, I met as a boy in Ireland in my native town, and instantly knew him for what he was . . . [35]

If it rejects the above explanation, what alternatives has psychology to offer? There are several. One psychological explanation is simply that we have already been to the place we now recognize but have forgotten doing so.

For example, a woman said: 'I spent a few days at the French Channel coast resort of Wimereux, near Boulogne, where I got the most intense feeling that I had been there before, although I couldn't remember having done so. I wasn't able to convince myself that I had been there until one day after returning from my holiday I came across by accident a very old hotel bill, which showed that I had spent a week there thirty years ago.'

Another explanation is that the present experience reminds you of some incident or situation which resembles it but which you have now forgotten. The present experience reawakens the memory of the previous experience buried in your unconscious mind. You thus feel as though you were recognizing something instead of experiencing it for the first time. The past experience has been largely forgotten, but the resemblance leads to the feeling that 'it has happened before'.

For example, a man and his wife were motoring through New England when they came to a village which he recognized as having seen before, although he knew and his wife agreed that he had never been there. The explanation was that when he was a child his family had had a maid who came from a farm near the village and who had talked incessantly to the boy about her home but he had forgotten it.

'The process of forgetting,' says Professor Edward Stevens Robinson of Yale University, 'sometimes leads us to recognize that which we have never before experienced. This is probably because we have experienced something like the happening in question, but have so nearly forgotten it that we are unable to tell the difference between the partially remembered happening and that which is falsely recognized.'

A third explanation is that what you now believe you have seen or done before is actually something which you have seen or done before in your imagination and which you have stored in your unconscious mind. The original fantasy of seeing or doing it has been repressed, so that you have remained unaware of it. The only evidence of its existence is the feeling of familiarity that now strikes you. This is created by the fact that you are now doing something which you have already imagined yourself doing.

For example, a soldier said: 'When I put on a black dress uniform and looked at myself in the mirror, I had a funny feeling as if I had done it before, yet I knew I hadn't.' The explanation was that about nine months previously he had imagined how smart he would look in such a uniform.

Freud accepts this explanation. He considers the *déjà vu* phenomenon to be based on the memory of an unconscious fantasy. The feeling of familiarity can be referred to fantasies of which we are unconsciously reminded in an actual situation.

For example, a woman told him that as a child of twelve she had visited the house of some friends in the country. There she was struck by the feeling that she had seen everything before, although she knew that this was the first visit she had paid to it. The explanation was that a few months before her visit she had had to leave home and stay with relatives on account of the illness of her only brother. Unconsciously she had hoped that when she returned home she would find that her brother had died and that she would be restored to the centre of the family stage. However, her brother did not die and the thought remained repressed. A few months later, when she visited the home of her friends, she found that their brother, too, was ill. This similarity between their home and her own revived the memory of her unconscious fantasy and created the sense of familiarity which she experienced.

'I believe,' writes Freud, 'that it is wrong to designate the feeling of having experienced something before as an illusion. On the contrary, in such moments, something is really touched that we have already experienced, only we cannot consciously recall the latter because it never was conscious. In the latter, the feeling of *déjà vu* corresponds to the memory of an unconscious fantasy.'[36]

When a long-past dream is stirred by some new occurrence, it, too, may cause this false recognition. For example, a man said: 'I get a feeling when I am in a strange place or faced with an unusual situation, that I have been there before, or coped with the situation before, when in reality I know I haven't! Would you infer that I have probably dreamed of this strange place or unusual situation at a previous date?'

The *déjà vu* experience occurs not only in waking life but it can also occur in dreams. This is illustrated by the following report of a woman who said: 'In my dreams I tend to get into situations which I feel I have been in before.'

The following dream throws light on the origin of the *déjà vu* experience. A young man said: 'I dreamed of a large house with a garden and a drive. I remembered it so vividly that I am sure I could recognize the place if I ever saw it.' If this young man were to forget this dream but later on to see a house which resembled the dream-house, he might well experience the feeling of familiarity characteristic of *déjà vu*.

(g) Shock

Shock, too, can be a cause of an impaired memory. It can be of two kinds. The first results from an intense emotional experience of a distressing nature.

'I received a sudden shock,' said Mr A. D. 'My memory then faded rapidly (almost, as far as I can remember, instantaneously). This led to doubt about what action I had taken in small things — and to loss of concentration.' He reported that this condition was still persisting nine years after the incident.

Mrs D. M. T. said: 'Three years ago my husband took early retirement. After thirty-five years of marriage, he used the lump sum he received from his firm to set up home with a lady out of his office. My mother, who had lived with us for twenty-three years, died of shock, and my memory is like a sieve. Sometimes when I'm holding a conversation with someone, I dry up and can't think what I was going to say.'

A Sunday newspaper reported the case of a man who found himself at Victoria Coach Station in London, having forgotten who he was. He was taken to Scotland Yard, where efforts were made to establish his identity. When they proved to no avail, the police referred to him temporarily as 'John Smith.' He told the newspaper: 'If you can help me to find out who I am, it will be a terrific relief. I suppose I must have had a shock of some kind. There was a lump on my head when the police saw me, but I remember nothing of being attacked. Since then I have had fits of depression trying to sort out this awful business.'

The following week the newspaper announced that, as a result of the publicity which it had given to the case, the man's identity had been established. His name was John F., who lived in Fleetwood. He reported: 'The police say that I am married and have a daughter and a son. I have been told I left home after a quarrel, but I can't remember anything about that.

'Fleetwood means nothing to me. It might as well have been Aberdeen or Cardiff, for all I know. My age is supposed to be fifty-six, but as far as I am concerned life began for me on the morning of New Year's Day, when I found myself in London and asked the police for help.'

The second kind of shock can result from treatment for nervous or mental illness. Some impairment of memory is a usual after-effect of electroconvulsive therapy (ECT). [37] The memory tends to recover spontaneously after the treatment has been discontinued. This is illustrated by the case of Mrs C. A. L., who reported: 'Eight years ago, after my son was born, I suffered from puerperal depression, resulting in a course of ECT at the local hospital. The treatment was completely successful and I have not suffered from depression again. I have overcome the loss of memory which the ECT produced.' This does not, however, always happen. For example, Mr J. H. B. said in 1982: 'In 1952 I had ECT. When you come to, you find that you have lost your memory, and if you don't regain it in a fortnight's time, you will not regain it at all. I can't even remember what I have done from day to day.'

5. Drugs

Drugs, whether taken with or without medical justification, can also be a cause of a poor memory.

'I am suffering from loss of memory,' said Mr. F. B. 'My doctor is treating me for high blood pressure, gastric ulcer, and a heart condition. I have to take a number of tablets, and my doctor tells me that these are the cause of my memory failure. My memory was normal in my school-days, when study was no trouble to me and I was always one of the top three in class.'

'As a soldier in the Nigerian civil war,' said Mr L. E., 'I took Indian hemp. This had no ill effect on me throughout the war. But now that it is over and I have gone back to school, the effect has come on remarkably. This has, in fact, retarded my ability to concentrate properly on my studies. Moreover, forgetfulness and absent-mindedness have become the chief aspects of my character now. Formerly I was very good at memorizing, especially poems and articles in newspapers and magazines, and I was above average in academic work. But since this unfortunate catastrophe my academic record has fallen. In fact, this has affected every aspect of my life. I'm greatly worried. I have reported my case to doctors in psychiatric hospitals, but after the use of the tablets they recommended there was no improvement.'

Formerly thought to be harmless, Indian hemp or marijuana or pot, as it is commonly known, has now been found to be damaging to the brain. The substances in it are soluble in fat and are attracted to the body's fatty organs, of which the brain is one. People can drink for years before serious brain damage shows, but it begins to develop in a relatively short time when marijuana is taken. Particularly noticeable is impairment of short-term memory; in chronic cases this may prove irreversible.

Here is another case with unusual features illustrating the effect of drugs on memory. 'When I was twenty-three,' said Mrs J. McG., 'the chemist gave me the wrong tablets. I was unconscious for two and a half months. When I regained consciousness, I had completely lost my memory, so much so that I couldn't even remember my own son. For nine years my memory was appalling. Then for some unknown reason it slowly but surely got better. Now I can remember the majority of things. But every so often I find I can't recall certain things.'

6. Smoking

'I learn quickly,' said Mrs E. C., 'and as quickly forget. I am worse than ever now as I have just given up smoking after over 50 years of it, sometimes smoking over 50 cigarettes a day. I just can't concentrate without a cigarette. I wish you could help me to forget my need of one!'

There is as yet no evidence that chronic heavy smoking is a cause of impaired memory. But it could well be. After all, the poisons that heavy smoking constantly pours into our bodies can, as H. M. Government frequently reminds us, seriously damage our health. Surely this includes the health of the brain and nervous system?

However, what seems to have happened in the above case is that Mrs E. C. has formed an association between smoking and concentration. Unless she is smoking, she is unable to concentrate. And, of course, as we have already established, impaired concentration is a common cause of a poor memory.

So, even if we leave aside the question of whether chronic heavy smoking has impaired this lady's memory, it seems clear that her concentration — and hence her memory — are suffering from the effects of her decision to give up smoking. One cannot escape the conclusion that she might have been wise not to take up smoking in the first place.

3.

How to Remember

Having established what the causes of forgetting are, we should now be in a position to suggest how they can be removed. Our conclusions on this point should yield us practical hints on making the most effective use of our memory. Incidentally, it should be mentioned, if it has not already been made clear, that what we learn here about both remembering and forgetting is not 'armchair' speculation. We are dealing with the scientific findings of psychologists based on their laboratory experiments.

First of all, let us recapitulate what we learned in Chapter 2. We discovered that the causes of forgetting are:

1. Getting a weak impression by not attending to an experience properly.
2. Letting the impression fall into disuse by failure to repeat it.
3. Interference from other impressions.
4. Repression of unpleasant memories.

This analysis shows us what we need to do to avoid or stop such causes. This is, in fact, all that the practical problem of memory amounts to. In order to reduce or remove the causes of forgetting and so be able to remember better, we have to:

1. Get a strong impression by paying careful attention.
2. Repeat under conditions in which repetition is effective.
3. Avoid or reduce interference as much as possible.
4. Lift the repression or avoid it forming.

It will be the purpose of the present chapter to try to show how each of these aims may be accomplished.

1. Impression

The first cause of a poor memory is getting a weak impression of the thing we wish to remember. Getting a strong impression of it means attending to it properly or concentrating on it.

We must obtain a deep impression on the mind of what we wish to remember. The attention must be concentrated on one thing only at a time to the exclusion of everything else.

At any given time various impressions converge upon the mind. A selection among them is effected by attention, which is the directing of mental activity towards a mental or physical object or situation. Attending to something consists in putting oneself into such a relation with it as to gain the fullest possible experience from it.

In every such mental process a certain amount of concentration is necessary. Concentration is, in fact, sustained attention. Hence we must understand certain facts about this process if we are to improve our power of concentration.

Attention is constantly shifting. Even when one is concentrating, attention shifts rapidly from one aspect to another of the matter to which we are attending. Some people claim to be able to carry on two or more activities at the same time. What really happens is that their attention changes continuously and rapidly from one to the other.

We cannot continue indefinitely to attend to one thing if no new focus of interest is introduced. If forced beyond this point, natural sleep or an hypnotic state ensues. This is, in fact, the principle which the hypnotist uses in putting his subject 'under the influence'.

We cannot concentrate on one object for any considerable length of time without an effort of will. When we listen to a monotonous speaker, our attention wanders to other matters and has to be recalled. A single object or situation cannot hold attention for very long unless it has many details, such as a painting. Thus a thought cannot usually be retained for a long time before other thoughts interrupt. This lack of constancy is found especially in children. In adults there are great individual differences with respect to it. These also depend on the kind of object observed and the individual interest in it.

The problem of attention and concentration is really the problem of habit. We must develop the habit of paying attention to what concerns us. With practice we can learn to disregard many things which at first strongly attract our attention. If we lived within the sound of the Niagara

Falls, we should probably learn in time to ignore it. We can also learn to pay attention to some things which might otherwise be neglected, e.g. the ticking of a clock in a room full of the buzz of conversation.

Attention may be voluntary or involuntary. Voluntary attention is the result of forming the habit of attending. It is directed towards an object or idea by one's own decision backed by an effort of will. Involuntary attention, on the other hand, is brought about by the intensity of the impression or by the interest which it arouses.

Voluntary attention is fixed by an effort of will on some object which does not in itself interest us. The interest lies in some indirect object, as, for example, when one studies a dull subject in order to pass an examination.

If you want to concentrate on something, you must feel that it matters to you. You must be interested in it. It must evoke your enthusiasm. The deeper and more permanent the interest the more sustained the attention.

Without the interest that brings involuntary attention, an effort of will is necessary. This is bound to mean some degree of tension. If, however, the tension is too strong, it will distract us from what we are trying to concentrate on. We must strike a balance between relaxation and tension.

The distribution of attention is inversely proportional to its intensity. That is to say, if we concentrate intently on one object, other objects are observed to a lesser degree. Concentration can be disturbed by distracting impressions, especially those of emotional value, the strength of which increases the distraction. For example, a teacher said: 'I have begun work for an Arts degree but find great difficulty in concentrating because of my self-consciousness which is always before me.'

It will thus be seen that the problem of concentration lies in (a) forming the habit of bringing the mind back every time it wanders; (b) acquiring a deep and permanent interest in the matter to which we are seeking to attend; (c) relaxing our tension until we are slightly braced up but not too much; and (d) settling any emotional problems which distract our attention from what we are doing.

In other words, concentration depends upon four things: Habit, Interest, Relaxation and Emotion. These points may be remembered by summarizing them in the word HIRE.

Before passing on to consider each of them in greater detail, we are now in a position to say something about the value of attention. This will be seen when we realize that attention is the first step in all the higher mental processes. Its selective nature enables us to construct an orderly world out of the mass of sense impressions. The shifting of attention greatly facilitates one's adjustment to the environment. As soon as one aspect of the environment is fully comprehended, one's attention almost invariably shifts to another.

The improvement of concentration is a benefit sometimes claimed to result from the use of a particular brand of advertised product. The psychologist, however, must struggle on with such techniques of improving concentration as he has found of value.

(a) Habit

The inability to concentrate is often a sign that a person is the victim of over-indulgence in fantasy, which, when conscious, takes the form of day-dreaming. The law of attention is that we can attend to only one thing at once. While we are attending to our fantasies, we cannot concentrate upon anything else.

Many people complain of 'lack of concentration' or 'bad memory'. It may at first sight appear that they are right, but in reality they are complaining about their day-dreams. These so engross their attention as not to permit concentration. To concentrate under these circumstances requires an effort of will to check unconscious fantasy that runs counter to what we are trying to study.

Another factor plays a role in this condition. Our day-dreams are, as a rule, emotionally charged. On the other hand, study material with its relatively low emotional charge is often unable to attract a great amount of our attention. The student, therefore, prefers to indulge in day-dreams. Because he does not attend to what he seeks to learn, he does not remember it, and, therefore, he believes that he has a poor memory. For example, a student said: 'I am above average in my studies, but my problem is that I lack concentration when reading. My mind wanders away on to thoughts of sex.'

This man's mind is distracted from what he wishes to attend to by fantasies arising from the pressure of his natural instincts. Whilst he is attending to his fantasies or day-dreams, he cannot concentrate upon the subject he is reading, and unless a person concentrates he cannot expect to remember.

On the other hand, it would be a mistake to think that concentration is the full answer to the problem of memory. That something more besides is necessary is illustrated by the following report. A man said: 'I find it difficult to remember things that have been said to me, although I concentrate on what I am being told at the time.' Nevertheless, it cannot be denied that concentration is essential to memory, even if other conditions must be met as well.

Concentration is a habit and habits are perfected by practice. William James said: 'There is no such thing as voluntary, sustained attention for more than a few seconds at a time. What is called sustained, voluntary attention, is a repetition of successive efforts which bring back the topic to the mind.'

We must persevere in trying to concentrate until we succeed. Habit is as strong a force for good as for ill. We should try to build up habits that are conducive to concentration. For instance, it helps to sit down to work at a definite time and in a definite place.

If your mind tends to wander to other things, bring it back gently each time to what you are doing. Other thoughts tend to intrude because this is the normal way in which the mind works, one thought succeeding another. The technique of concentrating 'goes against the grain' and may, therefore, require some practice before it succeeds. Persistent practice of this kind will eventually enable you to develop the habit of concentration.

When you find it hard to concentrate, the thoughts that crowd into your mind are not unimportant. If they push out what you are trying to study, they must be more important than the latter. In fact, they may contain a key to your most important problems. They may be your mind's way of advising you to 'put first things first'.

For example, a young teacher complained: 'I find it very hard to concentrate and apply myself properly to my studies.' Invited to give details of the thoughts that passed through his mind while studying, he replied: 'There is always some girl in my mind. I picture myself making advances to her. I think of myself in some heroic position with a girl admiring me.'

These thoughts show that the young man's real problem is not his difficulty in concentrating but his sexual frustration. The tendency to rely upon fantasy for compensation will diminish as his life situation brings him greater satisfaction in the world of reality. Always begin by dealing with your most important problem, and then you will find that concentration is no trouble at all.

(b) Interest

A man said: 'When I listen to a person talking to me about something uninteresting, my mind wanders. I want to improve my concentration. Can you tell me how?'

This report illustrates that concentration depends upon interest in what we are doing. This man's mind wanders from what is being said because, as he himself admits, he finds it uninteresting.

The law of interest is of paramount importance in concentrating. Interest means to be in the midst of a situation. Unless interest is present, unless one throws oneself heart and soul into a thing, concentration becomes extremely difficult or even impossible without a deliberate effort of will. And while the individual is attending to willing himself to concentrate, he cannot attend to what he is trying to concentrate on.

Interest is the pleasure derived from the harmonious coexistence of a present impression and one which has been perceived previously. This psychological process also arouses a sense of familiarity, and attention is then directed towards the impression, selecting it from a number of other objects.

The Queen's well-known interest in horses illustrates the dependence of memory upon this factor. In her book *Royal Horses* Judith Campbell says that Her Majesty has a 'photographic' memory for horses. People were amazed, she records, when, during a tour of Australia in 1977, the Queen was shown a stallion, Without Fear, and said that she remembered him, having seen him as a foal at a stud in Normandy ten years earlier. On another occasion the Queen picked out a newcomer, Doutelle, from two chestnut colts who arrived together and whose labels had been lost. She had originally seen him as a foal.

We must develop and build an interest in whatever we would mentally retain. Things in which we are deeply interested will be remembered without conscious effort. As a private secretary put it: 'I do not forget anything that is vital to me.'

For example, a boy who is interested in planes or trains easily recognizes the different types he spots because his interest has led him to study them. On the other hand, to the person who has no special interest in them one plane or locomotive looks very much like another.

Another example which illustrates the dependence of memory upon interest is the following. A man said: 'For certain things my memory is very good. Usually they are memories tied up with my interests. Some people are quite surprised on occasions when I can recall instances where they have either said or done something which they had forgotten. I can remember a colleague's surprise as she was going through a list of some musical shows and operatic works she had seen — but she had forgotten a rarer work which she definitely had seen — Bizet's "Pearl Fishers". It has been a few years since she had mentioned seeing this work but her interest in opera was not so keen as mine. It was therefore much to her surprise when I remembered something that was really part of her own memory.'

If we have to attend to something in spite of its being uninteresting, we can improve our concentration by strengthening our interest. This can be done in the following way. The practical remedy for the difficulty is to repeat to ourselves: 'This interests me and I'll remember it', or 'This work is interesting me more and more', or 'This subject is useful to me and I like it more each day'.

In other words, to stimulate interest where it is flagging, or to cultivate it where it is lacking altogether, make use of the simple method of autosuggestion. The value of this advice may be judged from the following reports made by persons who applied it and found it beneficial.

'This method has helped a lot to overcome my inability to concentrate,' said a student. 'Now when I read I take in about twice as much as I did previously.'

Another person who complained of lack of concentration reported: 'My power of concentration has greatly improved. When I was reading, my mind would just wander away, but now I can concentrate on a subject because it interests me.'

Concentration and memory, however, do not depend entirely upon interest. Interest by itself will not ensure a person being able to concentrate and remember. This may be noted from the following reports.

'I find great difficulty in remembering things I have read,' said a housewife, 'even though I take a great interest in them.'

'I don't seem as though I can concentrate,' said a salesman, 'no matter how hard I try. It's not because I am not interested. I am indeed full of enthusiasm about the work.'

This illustrates an important point about interest. One must really be interested in a thing *for its own sake* in order to be able to concentrate on it. This man was not really interested in his work for its own sake. His real difficulty was not lack of concentration but self-consciousness. He was interested in his work because he though that it promised him a means of convincing himself that he had overcome his self-consciousness.

Here are three further examples that illustrate this important point.

A woman said: 'I am tone-deaf. Apparently this slight physical defect has been with me all my life. It seems to me that owing to it I have never really listened properly to anything or anybody, and if I read my powers of concentration are not at all good. Do you think I could make myself listen to talks on the radio if I really concentrated?'

What she appears to be saying to herself is: 'If I listened to talks on the radio, it would prove that I was able to concentrate.' However, this is not the best motive for listening to radio talks. The proper motive for doing this is that you are interested in the subject of the talk.

A man said: 'I am studious-minded and have spent a lot on postal tuition, but whenever I try to study I fail to concentrate and fall asleep.'

This man may be trying to study because he thinks that success in that line would give him a good opinion of himself or give other people a good opinion of him. Such a motive, however, is not a satisfactory substitute for a genuine interest in the subject-matter of the lessons. This interest may be absent in his case and, if so, it would explain why he is unable to concentrate and tends to escape into sleep.

There are two ways of solving this problem. One is that he should give up his studies and find some other way of spending his time. The other is to cultivate a genuine interest in the actual subject-matter of the lessons. This can be attempted on the lines shown above.

Here is another example of a man who was doing the right thing for the wrong reasons. He said: 'I want to study for my GCE in five subjects, but find great difficulty in settling down and concentrating properly. I have been studying on and off for about five years, but have made little progress. I think that, because I did not get my School Certificate at school, I have had a secret inferiority complex. If I had some qualification, it would be a spur to further ambition.'

His real problem is that he feels inferior. He no doubt believes that if he were to obtain his GCE, it would give him a better opinion of himself. It would enable him to feel the equal of or even superior to some other people who do not possess the GCE.

The snag is that this motive will not in itself sustain his studies of five subjects. He can do this only if he is interested in the subjects for their own sake. If you are going to study, say, English Literature or Mathematics or French, you must have a keen interest in these branches of knowledge themselves. This may be what he lacks and, if so, it explains his difficulty in getting down to his studies.

In other words, you should study algebra, or Latin or history, or whatever it is, because you think that they are worth studying — not because of what you think the possession of GCE can do for you.

If he can discover within himself a genuine interest in his subjects as subjects, this man should be able to obtain his GCE. On the other hand, if he is not interested in the subjects for their own sake, he would be wise to get into some other occupation where he can made progress without possessing a GCE.

(c) Relaxation

What is the relation between concentration and relaxation? Is concentration assisted by relaxing or by tensing? This seems to be a matter of debate.

One opinion favours the view that concentration occurs most naturally when body and mind are relaxed. According to this view, the ideal means of concentrating would be to sit down in a relaxed posture. That is to say, the person who is concentrating is not all keyed up and tense, but relaxed and confident.

For example, a bank clerk said: 'I make mistakes because I am trying too hard to concentrate. I find it very difficult to concentrate at all, as I am unable to relax. I think it would be a great help if I were.'

Relaxation should not, of course, be confused with fatigue. Little is gained by attempting to concentrate when one is tired. 'My main trouble is overwork,' said a forty-year-old widow. 'When I do sit down to study I am too tired to concentrate.'

On the other hand, there are those who favour the view that concentration means tension, not relaxation. Jacobsen, author of *Progressive Relaxation,* states that mental activity in general diminishes as muscular relaxation progresses. 'With progressive muscular relaxation,' he writes, 'attention, thought-processes, and emotion gradually diminish.' He concludes that 'the experience of muscular tenseness' is a necessary requirement of attention.[38]

Muensterberg, too, believed that concentration demands muscular tension. He formulated what is known as the action theory, which maintains that the strength of our attention, or perhaps better, its vividness, when looking at an object, for example, depends on the openness of the paths in the nervous system leading to the muscles. When these paths are not wholly clear, the object we are perceiving or the words we are listening to will not register fully in consciousness. To attend will, therefore, require a certain muscular tension or preparedness.

Robert H. Thouless advocates 'a position in which the muscles are braced up' as favourable to concentration. Yet he admits that 'keeping the muscles tense is not the same thing as mental concentration and is not even essential to it, and it has the objection that it is fatiguing in itself.'

This controversy on the merits of relaxation versus tension for concentration has now been settled by Courts.

In Courts's experiment sixty college students learned nonsense syllables while exerting muscular effort by squeezing a dynamometer. A nonsense syllable consists of a vowel between two consonants, e.g. zek. A dynamometer is an instrument designed to measure strength of grip. Each subject squeezed the dynamometer as hard as he could in order to measure the strength of his maximum grip. Then he learned lists of syllables both without squeezing the dynamometer and also while squeezing it at different strengths up to his maximum grip. When the subjects were tested on how much they had learned, it was shown that the number of syllables which they recalled increased up to the point where they were exerting a quarter of their maximum grip. Beyond that point the number of syllables recalled began to fall off, until by the time they were exerting three-quarters of their maximum grip they actually recalled less than they did without the dynamometer at all.

The conclusion to be drawn from this experiment is that *a slight amount of tension improves learning, but a larger amount diminishes it.*[39]

(d) Worry or Emotional Conflict

A young man said: 'I find difficulty in concentrating. Whenever I am reading or attending lectures, my mind wanders. I am beginning to worry about it, because, unless I put all my mind into my work, there are scant chances of passing examinations.'

'The normal person concentrates on what seems to him important,' says Freud, 'in the way of an impression or a piece of work in order that it shall not be interfered with by the intrusion of any other mental processes or activities.'[40]

When it is interfered with, as in the above case, this is often a sign that a person is the victim of emotional conflict. This more than anything else interferes with the process of sustained attention.

The *law of attention,* which we noted earlier, is that *one cannot attend to two things at once,* or that *two or more things cannot be done with equal intensity.* A man reading his programme as he watches a play seems to be able to attend to both at the same time. The truth of the matter, however, is that his attention alternates rapidly between the two.

The inability to attend may be due to worry about one's other problems. While you are attending to your problems or worries, you cannot concentrate upon anything else. For example, of a group of college students who were referred for psychiatric aid on account of reading disabilities, half were found to have emotional difficulties. The most common included feelings of inferiority and insecurity, immature personalities, depression and poor social adaptation.[41]

This means that lack of concentration may not be the main problem. It may merely point to the existence of some other problem that requires to be solved. When this has been done, there should be no further difficulty in concentrating, for the attention will then no longer be divided between the worrying problem and the effort to concentrate.

The truth of this statement is borne out time and again by persons who at first complain of being unable to concentrate and afterwards admit that they don't like their jobs or that some other difficulty needs to be put right.

For example, a student who at first submitted lack of concentration as his problem, was afterwards found to be a partner to a broken marriage. When he had solved his marital difficulties, his inability to concentrate disappeared without requiring to be treated as a separate problem.

A man complained: 'I am hampered by a poor power of concentration. I cannot keep my mind from wandering.' Later he made the following disclosure: 'Actually it was a case of worrying. When you state that my lack of concentration is due to emotional conflict, you are perfectly correct. I am living with a woman for whom I have not the slightest affection. We have a boy of two to whom I am devoted. My lawful wife, whom I deserted, is prepared to take me back. I want to return to her but cannot leave my baby, whom the mother will not give to me.'

Another man also complained of difficulty in concentrating. His real problem, which he did not reveal until fifteen months later, was that he was a homosexual. 'I was a fool,' he admitted, 'to think that any problem was too private to disclose, or too antisocial for you to attend to, and so I kept quiet about the one serious problem I had and still have.'

The principle that the student should follow for improving his concentration is to seek out and remove the real difficulty responsible for it, and not to expect to be able to concentrate until he has done so. You should face up to your emotional problems, and do what you can to solve them if they can be solved, or accept them and learn to live with them if they cannot be solved.

The fourth rule for improving one's powers of concentration is, therefore, to attend either to the matter in hand, or, if that is not possible, to one's worries with a view to eliminating them, but do not expect to be able to attend to both at once.

Summary of Advice on How to Concentrate

Let us now summarize what we have learned about the causes of poor concentration and how to eliminate them. We have learned that lack of concentration is caused by the habit of day-dreaming, lack of interest in the subject, too little or too much muscular tension, and worry or emotional conflict, which distracts attention from what we are doing.

This means that we must acquire the habit of concentration by bringing our mind back every time it wanders to other things. We must strengthen our interest in the subject by repeating to ourselves, 'This work is interesting me more and more'. A slight degree of muscular tension is needed, but not too much. The ideal means of concentrating is to sit down in a lightly braced posture. Finally, we should try to deal with any emotional problems that we have. A quiet mind is the best guarantee of concentration.

In overcoming inattention we learn to concentrate. We thus deal with the first cause of a poor memory, i.e. the original experience not making a strong enough impression on us. Better concentration means a stronger impression, and the more vivid the impression the easier it is recalled.

Before passing on to consider the second cause of a poor memory and what can be done to eradicate it, we must note that the attention we are asked to give should be active and not passive, i.e., we should make a definite resolve to remember what we are paying attention to.

Attending without actively resolving to remember is of little use. For example, a man said: 'I remembered a person quite well — his voice, the circumstances of our meeting, etc., but not his name, for I did not make any serious attempt to commit his name to memory at the time.'

A psychologist was able to memorize a list of nonsense syllables after repeating them only nine times, when he made up his mind to learn them. When he did not make up his mind to learn them but merely repeated them parrot fashion (passive attention), he required eighty-nine repetitions to memorize a similar list. [42]

Another man recalled the following memory, which at the time of its occurrence had been accompanied by the intention to remember it:

'One winter, when I was about eight, I was sledging in the late evening down a slope outside our house. The pleasure was such that I wished it would never end. The only flaw in my happiness was the certain knowledge that one of my parents would shortly come to the gate and call me in. As I careered downhill for the umpteenth time, I became aware that I had a spectator. My father was standing at the gate. He smiled but did not call me. I went downhill twice more and then made for the gate, my sledge bumping up the steps after me. As we went in together I thought: "I will always remember this evening," and I always have.'

A woman said: 'I cannot remember book titles very well unless I make a special effort. If I read a book which I am not likely to pick up again, I have no sooner put it down than the title has gone from me. It is the same with films.'

This experience, too, illustrates the part played in remembering by the resolve to remember. She did not remember the title of a book or film because, not being interested in reading or seeing it again, she did not make a conscious resolve to remember it.

Therefore, don't be content merely to attend to what you are doing, but study it with the conscious intention to remember it. Make up your mind that you will remember it. Memory is assisted by the intention to remember. What you will to remember you actually do remember.

2. Repetition

In an experimental proof of the effectiveness of repetition a number of radio scripts were prepared in two versions. In one version the material was presented straightforwardly without repetition. In the other the main points were repeated several times. Both versions were read to each group of the audience taking part in the experiment. After each script had been read the members of the audience answered questions on its factual content and were also asked to say how well they had understood the passage.

When the main points of a script were repeated the material was both understood and remembered better than when there was no repetition. 'Repetition facilitates comprehension and aids memory,' conclude the authors of the experiment. [43]

We have noted that attention is most effective when accompanied by the resolve to remember. There are also certain conditions under which repetition is most effective. Merely repeating what we wish to remember does not in itself ensure that we remember it, although, of course, we cannot be expected to remember it unless we do repeat it.

Psychologists have discovered a number of conditions under which repeating what we wish to remember helps us to remember it. Some of these conditions, which we will examine in the present section, are as follows:

(a) You remember better if you understand what you repeat. (Comprehension.)

(b) You remember better if you study a little but often. (Spaced learning.)

(c) You remember better if you recite to yourself. (Recitation.)

(d) You remember better if you repeat for longer than you need to learn. (Overlearning.)

(e) You remember better if you repeat wholes rather than parts. (Whole learning.)

(f) You remember better if you tell yourself that you can. (Autosuggestion.)

(g) You remember better under conditions like those under which you learned. (Reintegration.)

(h) You remember uncompleted tasks better than completed ones. (Zeigarnik effect.) This holds true unless you are afraid of failure or concerned about success, when you may remember a completed task better than an uncompleted one.

(i) You remember better something that contrasts with its background. (von Restorff effect.)

Let us describe and illustrate each of these conditions in turn.

(a) The Law of Comprehension (Memory and Meaning)

What is the law of comprehension? It is: to remember — understand. The law states a fact of common experience. This is that the better we understand what we learn, the better we remember it. Meaningful material is better retained or more readily relearned than nonsense or rote material. The more meaning any material has the more easily it is memorized and the less rapidly it is forgotten. For example, Ebbinghaus showed that, after they had been learned, relatively fewer repetitions were required to relearn eighty-syllable stanzas of 'Don Juan' than to relearn a twelve-syllable nonsense list. [44] A conscious intention must be made to memorize relatively meaningless material. This is just as well; otherwise our minds would be cluttered with useless information.

You can make practical use of this law if you clearly comprehend what you want to remember; if the meaning is not clear it is difficult to remember it. The very effort to find a meaning will stimulate attention and fix the material more firmly in the memory. 'The more you know about a thing,' writes Dr Henry Knight Miller in *Practical Psychology*, 'the easier it is to remember. *Always try to understand.* '[45]

Try to gain insight into the general principles that govern the skill or knowledge you wish to acquire. Keep your mind open for new meanings. If you fail to see them, however, put the problem on one side. You cannot force a solution and prolonged 'trial and error' is wasteful. Return to the problem later on when insight may come with little effort.

Thorndike formulated the above principle in another way as the law of belongingness, which states that items integrated into a pattern are better remembered than those which merely occur in close proximity. Christian names and surnames, for example, appear to 'go together' and may be better learned than a series of pairs of Christian names. Subjects and predicates go together. The law of belongingness also refers to seeing the relations between the part and the whole

The value of comprehension is underlined by the following experiment. Two classes of pupils were asked to learn these numbers:

581215192226

293336404347

The first class was told that both numbers were built up on the same principle and that they could remember the numbers by discovering the principle. The principle is that of adding 3 and then 4, i.e., 5 plus 3 = 8, 8 plus 4 = 12, etc.

Then the second class was told to learn the numbers by grouping them in threes and they were written on the blackboard in the following fashion:

| 581 | 215 | 192 | 226 |
| 293 | 336 | 404 | 347 |

Twenty-three per cent of Class I, who had memorized by understanding, were able to remember both numbers correctly three weeks later, while not one of the second class was able to do so.

This clearly shows that we remember best what has meaning for us, or, at least, we may remember it better than what has little or no meaning for us.[46]

(b) *Spaced Learning ('Little and Often')*
Which is the better method of studying a correspondence course — thirty minutes every day or two hours every three or four days?

The better method is to spend thirty minutes every day. A short period of study each day is better than a longer period every now and then.

Ebbinghaus found that material which he learned by practice spaced over several days was better remembered than material learned by practice massed on one day.[47]

Mr S. L. said: 'I study only at weekends because during the week I am too busy.' It must be admitted that this is not an ideal method of study. After a week he has probably forgotten most of what was studied the previous weekend.

Instead of spending an hour or two once a week he would do better to spread the same time over seven days. This helps to keep the material fresh in mind and to get the best out of one's studies. This man did, in fact, adopt the suggestion. Up to that point his average mark per lesson for his written work had been 77 per cent. After his attention had been drawn to the value of spaced learning, his average mark per lesson rose to 92 per cent.

'As in music, which I am also studying,' he added, 'daily practice should be the rule, and from now on I intend to make time for it.'

In a psychological experiment, substituting letters for numbers was memorized nearly twice as well in six twenty-minute periods as in one period of two hours. One hundred and thirty-five letters were substituted for numbers in the two-hour practice period as compared with 195 letters in three forty-minute periods, 255 letters in six twenty-minute periods, and 265 letters in twelve ten-minute periods. In other words, when the same amount of time was broken up or spaced into six practice periods, the results were almost twice as good as in one period. [48]

Another experiment compared three methods of spacing twenty-four repetitions of lists of nonsense syllables. When the learners were tested, six repetitions a day for four days yielded a higher score than eight repetitions a day for three days. A still higher score was achieved, however, from two repetitions a day for twelve days. That is to say, the longer the period over which the repetitions were spaced, the greater the amount that was remembered. [49]

'Similar work has also been done with sensible material — prose or poetry — to be learned,' writes Dr Francis Aveling; 'and the same general advantage of "spaced out" over continuous learning has been established here.'

In acquiring a skill, too, daily practice is superior to longer but less frequent practice. This is illustrated by an experiment in which drawing a star while looking in a mirror was mastered better in short daily periods than in longer periods on alternate days. A psychologist compared the progress made by two groups of people. One group practised once at each sitting, which was held every day. The other group practised ten times at each sitting, which was held every other day. At the end of a week the first group had made the same progress as the second group, although the first had practised only seven times as compared with the other group's thirty attempts. [50, 51]

Suppose one is going to have, say, a course of ten driving lessons. Imagine that they are being taken by a person who as yet has no car of his own. Therefore, he will not be getting any practice in the intervals between the lessons. Is it better for him to have one lesson a week for ten weeks or one lesson a day for ten days? In either case he will do the same amount of driving and the cost will be the same. The sole criterion by which to judge between the two methods is the efficiency with which the skill is mastered.

The principle of spaced learning argues in favour of the daily lessons being the more efficient procedure for our learner-driver. In the once-weekly method the skill acquired at each lesson will be largely lost in the intervals between lessons. By contrast, the daily lessons will reinforce that skill before it has time to fall into disuse. Therefore, if practicable, the daily method is to be preferred.

(c) *The Law of Recitation*

The law of recitation states that study material is learned more rapidly when it is recited to oneself or aloud at frequent intervals during memorizing.

Instead of continued re-reading of a lesson it is better to recite to yourself what you have learned before you have finished learning it. Interrupt your reading in order to run over what you have learned either by mentally recapitulating the main points or preparing a written summary.

Recitation of the material during learning increases the amount which will be remembered. 'If I can read it out aloud,' said Miss D. S., 'I find it sinks in better.'

Why is it better to repeat the material aloud than to rely exclusively on silent reading? There are four reasons: (a) it makes the work more interesting; (b) it makes us pay more attention to it; (c) it enables us to test ourselves; and (d) it utilizes the ear, which is as much an aid to learning as the eye.

A well-known laboratory experiment in which students memorized short biographies which they afterwards reproduced has shown that memory is improved when as much as four-fifths of the study time is spent in mentally running over the material without referring to it. Sixty-two per cent of the material was remembered when four-fifths of the learning time was spent in recalling what had been learned in the remaining one-fifth, as against 46 per cent when the whole of the learning period was devoted to reading. [52]

By means of a film strip groups of recruits at a US Army reception centre were taught the phonetic alphabet, e.g., 'Able, Baker' for 'A, B,' etc. Half of the groups recited what they were learning by calling out the phonetic equivalents when they were shown the letters. The other half did no recitation by calling out, but were simply shown the letters with their equivalents. When both groups were tested the former remembered the material better than the latter. [53]

In other experiments on the learning of spelling, arithmetic and French vocabulary the self-recitation method has been proved to be much superior to merely studying and re-studying the material without reciting it. [54,55]

Reading and re-reading, then, although the commonest, is not the best method of study. It uses only the eye. If you want to remember better, you should use the ear and the muscle sense as well. This can be done by reading aloud or discussing what you read with another person. The muscle sense can be used by making notes on what you read and rewriting the notes, reorganizing them in different ways.

A student found lectures interesting, but missed a good deal while taking notes. He therefore decided to prepare a mental outline, writing up the lecture later. This form of recitation enabled him to memorize it.

Another example of the effective use of recitation is as follows. A young law student used to read newspaper reports of trials and then summarize them several times from memory. Each time he would compare his summary with the report, correcting and amending it until he was satisfied he knew it. Eventually he was able to remember the report of a trial after reading it only once. [56]

Dr Bruno Furst recommends that a similar method be used for learning geography. Draw from memory, he says, a map of a country. Correct your effort after comparing it with an atlas. Again draw the map from memory. Again correct it. When you are satisfied with your map, let a few days pass and then draw another one from memory.

(d) *The Law of Overlearning*
A very good principle to adopt is that of overlearning the material you are studying. Say it over and over again to yourself silently and aloud until you can repeat it several times without making a mistake.

The law of overlearning states that the more thoroughly study material is learned, the longer it is remembered. Material well learned is remembered better than material poorly learned. *Do not repeat what you wish to remember until you barely know it, but until you know it really well.*

A helpful point in remembering a chapter of a book is to go over the outstanding facts in one's mind after closing the book. Think about the subject-matter with a view to reconciling it with what you have learned previously and logically arranging it in your mind for future reference. Adopt the habit of frequently revising the material you have learned. For example, a student reports: 'I go over my lessons time and again till I have learned them off by heart.'

The simplest method of remembering names employs this principle of overlearning. Whenever you meet someone, get his or her name correctly. Give your full attention to it when you are introduced. Ask the person to repeat or spell it if you don't catch it the first time. Make a point of repeating the name several times during the course of conversation. For example, don't just say 'How do you do?'; say 'How do you do, Mrs Postlethwaite?'. Give yourself an incentive to remember their names by taking an interest in people. Associate a particularly difficult name with something else which you can remember. For example, a man whose name was Altkastell invited his friends to think of him as 'Oldcastle'.

When you think you have memorized a fact, it will repay you to go on repeating it a little longer. You remember a thing better if you continue to study it even after you have thoroughly learned it. Whatever time you spend on learning something, spend half as much time again on overlearning it. Something you learn in ten minutes will be remembered better if you repeat it for another five minutes after you know it.

A group of students repeated lists of nouns until they knew them. Another group repeated them for half as long again. After two weeks the latter group remembered more than four times as much as the former.

The degree of improvement in memory, however, is not uniformly proportional to the number of extra repetitions. A smaller number of extra repetitions is bound to result in an improvement. The further improvement from a large number of repetitions may not justify the time and effort spent on them, unless the material must be remembered perfectly, e.g. when a pianist practises for a concert. [57,58]

(e) The Law of Whole Learning

Generally speaking, material to be learned should be studied as a whole rather than bit by bit.

You will remember something better if you repeat it as a whole over and over again than if you break it up into parts and learn each part separately. The best way to memorize a passage is to keep reciting it in its entirety rather than a few lines at a time. Start with the whole but watch for spots that may call for special attention. Select for special practice the parts that are most difficult to learn. If the passage is very long, it should be divided into sections and each section treated as a whole.

For example, learn a poem as a whole rather than one stanza at a time. Read it all through and through until it is mastered rather than divide it into parts and memorize the parts before trying to recite the whole. In the case of poems up to 240 lines in length, the saving of time by the whole method of reading the complete poem through each time may amount to as much as 15 per cent. After the part method of learning a poem verse by verse we must mentally put the whole together at the end; reading the whole poem also adds meaning to the learning.

That is why in learning to play the piano students practise both hands together instead of each hand separately, and why the swimmer practises arm and leg movements together.

Seibert compared two ways of studying French vocabulary: to read through and through the list of words from beginning to end (whole method), or study it a word at a time (part method). When she compared the results of both methods, she found that students who had adopted the former remembered after two days half as much again as students who had studied one word and its French equivalent at a time. [59]

The superiority of the whole method over the part method of learning is further illustrated by the way in which the training of Morse code operators was improved in the United States army during World War II. Originally the code had been taught by the part method, in which the letters of the alphabet and the ten numerals were learned in several groups. The psychologists who were asked to improve the training recommended that the code be learned as a whole. As a result of this and other improvements the rate of failure among soldiers undergoing training was reduced from 15 per cent to 3.4 per cent, and the time required for training radio operators was reduced from between thirty-five and forty-one hours to twenty-seven hours. [60]

My daughter has shown me a religious tract in which the reader is recommended to memorize four scriptural texts as follows: learn the first, then learn the second and revise the first. When you have memorized the first two, learn the third. When you have learned the first three, learn the fourth. It is obvious that this is the part method. The material would probably be learned quicker and remembered better if all four texts were learned together, the reader repeating them all one after the other until they were known.

(f) The Law of Confidence

A poor memory can be caused by constantly telling ourselves that our memory is poor.

An attitude of confidence in one's memory tends to make it better than it would otherwise be. Fear, self-consciousness, stage-fright and worry interfere with the process of recalling.

Four patients were told under hypnosis, 'You will forget everything about your body when you awaken.' Not only were they unable to name parts of their bodies but one patient, for example, found it difficult to name objects and to draw geometrical figures. Another was unable to recognize articles of clothing, and estimated wrongly the length, thickness and parallelism of lines. This study illustrates in a striking way how responsive our memory is to the suggestion that it is poor. If we accept such a suggestion, it will actually tend to make our memory poor. [61]

You can improve your confidence in your memory by means of autosuggestion, repeating to yourself, 'Day by day in every way, I remember better and better.' Repeat this formula twenty or thirty times when you retire at night, after placing a ticking clock by your bedside. When you grow drowsy, turn your attention to the clock and go to sleep hearing its ticking say, 'I remember better — I remember better.'

'Demand good service of your memory,' writes William Walker Atkinson, 'and it will learn to respond. Learn to trust it, and it will rise to the occasion. How can you expect your memory to give good service when you continually abuse it and tell everyone of ''the wretched memory I have; I can never remember anything''? Your memory is very apt to accept your statements as truth; our mental faculties have an annoying habit of taking us at our word in these matters. Tell your memory what you expect it to do; then trust it and refrain from abusing it and giving it a bad name . . . Our advice is to get acquainted with your memory, and make friends with it. Treat it well and it will serve you well.'[62]

(g) *Reintegration*

We remember better if certain conditions present at the time of learning are also present when we try to remember what we have learned. We tend to forget because we try to recall something in circumstances different from those in which we learned it.

When the original conditions of learning are reinstated, remembering is enhanced. This is why it is often helpful when we want to recall something we have forgotten, to retrace our steps and repeat what we were doing when we originally committed the fact to memory.

For example, a man said: 'I find that as I lie down in bed I recall a dream of the previous night.' He recalled because lying down in bed reinstated the conditions under which he originally experienced the dream.

Again, reintegration occurs when, for instance, we go from one room to fetch something from another room. On arrival there we find that we have forgotten what we went for and in order to remember we have to go back to our starting point and remind ourselves what it was we wanted. Before we can remember we have to reinstate the original conditions under which the resolve to fetch the thing was formed.

This principle is an argument in favour of study taking place each day at the same time. You should sit at the same table or desk in the same room with your books arranged in the same way.

Another application of this principle is that a foreign language should be studied in a setting which resembles as closely as possible that in which it will be used. As Stuart Chase points out in *Guides to Straight Thinking*, words are meaningless unless they can be related to the experience of the speaker and the hearer.[63] This is the basic principle of all language study. From it stems the practical corollary that a foreign language is best learned by living in the country in which it is used. Of course, this is not practicable for all students of foreign languages. In that case the next best thing is to learn in a situation which reproduces as nearly as possible the conditions of the foreign setting.

For example, this is where radio can help; the listener to the BBC series of language broadcasts can overhear French or German voices in a French or German setting, and thus associate directly in his mind the French or German way of saying things with the situation in which they are heard. This is in fact the surest way of learning to speak a language.

(h) *Memory for Completed and Uncompleted Tasks (Zeigarnik Effect)*
Another discovery of practical value is that an uncompleted task is remembered better than a completed one.

'A failure makes one inventive,' wrote Freud, 'creates a free flow of associations, brings idea after idea, whereas once success is there a certain narrow-mindedness or thick-headedness sets in.'[64]

'This is a finding,' writes Dr Robert H. Thouless in *General and Social Psychology,* 'which has implications for the practical educator who may reflect on the danger of too early and complete explanation in the process of teaching leaving no tensions to aid remembering.'[65]

It means that you should arrange to break off your studies just before you come to the end of a natural division of the subject-matter. If we break off our studies before we have finished a chapter, we shall remember the material better when we return to it later.

Remembering uncompleted tasks better than completed ones is known as the Zeigarnik effect from the name of the German woman psychologist who discovered it in 1927. It is based on the following experiment.

Subjects were given about twenty tasks, such as modelling animals, stringing beads and solving puzzles, half of which were allowed to be completed, but the other half were interrupted.

After the experiment the subjects were asked to list all the things they had done. It was found that the uncompleted tasks were remembered much more frequently than the completed ones in spite of the fact that a longer time was generally spent on the completed than on the uncompleted tasks.[66]

Baddeley found a Zeigarnik effect, too, in an experiment in which he interrupted subjects who were attempting to solve anagrams by telling them the solution.[67]

Ovsiankina showed that the Zeigarnik effect disappears if the subjects are allowed to complete the uncompleted tasks. [68]

Kurt Lewin has attempted a theoretical explanation by postulating that to begin an activity of any kind creates a tension which persists until that activity is finished and accounts for the uncompleted activity being retained in memory.

Experiments which have been performed by other psychologists have qualified the results obtained by Zeigarnik. More recent evidence indicates that the Zeigarnik effect applies only to memory for tasks performed without emotional stress. Although people differ widely in this respect, it has been found that, where a person feels that not completing the task threatens his self-esteem, or in other ways places him under emotional stress, the opposite trend occurs. That is to say, when a person is labouring under emotional stress, a completed task is remembered better than an uncompleted one.

The practical application of this principle is that, if you are worried about getting through your work, you will remember what you read better by finishing the chapter than by not finishing it. On the other hand, if you are not worried, you will remember better by breaking off before you complete the chapter.

In such cases it would seem that the tendency to suppress unpleasant memories is stronger than the Zeigarnik effect, thus making it easier to recall the completed than the uncompleted task.

The Zeigarnik effect is illustrated by the following experience. 'I have studied only six lessons,' said a student. 'I want to complete the course. Unless I can do this I shall continue to have a feeling of something left undone. The unfinished thing is never attractive and I feel it is a nagging wound.'

Here is another illustration. A woman went to church when she was too poor to put anything in the collection plate. Soon afterwards she moved away from the neighbourhood and ceased to attend that particular church. But the incident continued to trouble her. Years later, when her circumstances had improved, she sent the rector a cheque for £25 with a note which said that she had felt guilty for many years and wished to make good her omission. This is another example of an uncompleted task being well remembered.

Should failure be associated with a completed task instead of with an uncompleted one, the Zeigarnik effect is reversed. That is to say, the completed task is then remembered better. This is illustrated by the following experiment.

The experimenter told the subject that some tasks were easy and others hard and that he was not concerned about the hard ones. If he saw that the subject was getting along well he would interrupt him, because the experimenter had learned all he needed to know. If the subject was not doing well, the experimenter would let him continue because then he needed to know how long it took to finish the task. Interruption thus became a sign of success and completion a sign of failure. Under these conditions the completed tasks were remembered better than the uncompleted ones. [69]

Atkinson also studied the effect of a person's concern for achievement on his ability to remember completed and uncompleted tasks. Three types of test situation were arranged: a relaxed, informal situation; an atmosphere created by the giving of instructions; and a situation in which the testee was urged to do his best, the result being regarded as a measure of intellectual ability, leadership, etc. It was found that more completed tasks were recalled as the atmosphere of the test situation increased from relaxed to ego-involved. This applied also to the uncompleted tasks — for persons with a high concern for achievement. However, persons with only a moderate concern for achievement remembered fewer uncompleted tasks as the situation changed from relaxed to tense. In other words, such persons regard their inability to complete a task as a failure which they prefer not to remember, while persons with a high concern for achievement regard the uncompleted tasks as challenges which they remember better in order to be able to complete them. The general conclusion is that we remember uncompleted tasks better when we have the positive goal of attaining success than we do when we have the negative goal of avoiding failure. [70]

Rosenzweig experimented with the solving of jigsaw puzzles by students, who were told that the puzzles were tests of intelligence and had to be completed in a certain time, otherwise they would be removed. Some of the puzzles were allowed to be completed while others were interrupted before they were finished. The students were encouraged to do their best in the available time.

It was found that the completed puzzles were remembered better than the uncompleted ones, the former being associated with a sense of achievement, the latter with failure. [71]

An uncompleted task is better remembered than a completed one when a person is interested in the task for its own sake and does not think of success as a boost to his self-esteem or of failure as a threat to it (task-oriented). On the other hand, a completed task is better remembered than an uncompleted one when a person works at it because of what it can do for him, because he regards success as necessary to his self-esteem but is not interested in the work for its own sake (ego-oriented).

This illustrates the fact that material connected with a pleasant feeling is better remembered than that associated with an unpleasant one. Once again we see that memory is not merely a passive process in which material that has been learned fades away wtih the passage of time. Indeed, as we noted in Chapter 2, Freud explained forgetting as due to an active process of repression which prevents the emergence into consciousness of ideas that are unacceptable to the ego. Our attention is, as it were, turned away from such ideas.

(i) *Figure and Ground (von Restorff Effect)*

A thing is remembered better if it contrasts with its background than if it blends with it. If some prankster lets off a firework in the middle of a symphony concert, the audience may remember the explosion better than some passage which occurs in the music. If I see the great white gash of a stone quarry in the Derbyshire hills, I remember this feature of the scene because it stands out from its background of the green countryside.

In the jargon that psychologists are fond of this is known as the *von Restorff effect*. Can it be turned to practical use in the task of learning? The answer is: Yes, it not only can but is so used. For example, when something is put in *italics* in a book, the *italic* print stands out in contrast with its background of roman print. The author uses this device because he wants to call your attention to the importance of the word, phrase or sentence. He hopes that by his so doing you will remember it better.

Even if what is important on a page is not italicized, you can still make it stand out by underlining it. If the book is your own you can do this as you read it and you can refresh your memory by revising the underlined passages.

But the device is also of value in less obvious ways. For example, why do some workers in industry like 'music while you work'? The more superficial answer is that it helps to relieve the monotony of their repetitive tasks. Might not an equally valid reason be that the details of the job are remembered better because they contrast with the background of the music?

Is 'music while you work' a help to students or merely a hindrance? Some students do indeed report that they can study better to the accompaniment of a background of music. The von Restorff effect explains why this is so. The material for study stands out by contrast against the musical background and may well be remembered better for that reason.

Of course, the musical background mustn't be such as to distract attention from the work. It must remain a background and no more. Therefore, it should for preference be one that is uninterrupted by pauses, without words to the music, and without startling contrasts in the type of music itself. Otherwise it may be more of a hindrance than a help to a person who is trying to study.

A neutral background can be used in the same way in other sense modalities. Why do tea-tasters or wine-tasters rinse their mouths out after each taste? The answer is that they remember the flavour of the tea or wine best if they perceive it against a neutral taste background than if it blends with other tastes still on the tongue.

What about the sense of touch or temperature? If we put a cold hand in hot water the water is remembered as being hotter than if we put the hand in hot water after taking it out of tepid water. Again the hot sensation contrasts more strongly with the cold background than with the tepid one and therefore is remembered better.

The von Restorff effect, then, defines the relationship of figure and ground in terms of the memorability of the former. A thing is remembered better if it contrasts with its background than if it blends with it.

To conclude this section let us remind ourselves again of the practical hints we have discovered for dealing with the second cause of forgetting, i.e. inadequate repetition. They are:

1.   *Make sure that you understand what you want to remember.*
2.   Study a little and often rather than a lot but seldom.
3.   *Recite the material to yourself aloud or silently.*

4. Repeat the material for longer than it takes just to know it.
5. *Learn by wholes rather than by parts.*
6. *Have confidence in your ability to remember.*
7. Conditions like those in which you learned help you to remember.
8. Uncompleted tasks are more easily remembered than completed ones (unless you are afraid of failure or concerned about success, when you may remember a completed task better than an uncompleted one).
9. Something that contrasts with its background is more easily remembered than something which blends with it.

The above principles have been tested and proved in the psychological laboratory. The value of four of them (the ones in italics) was convincingly shown in the following experiment which also illustrated the importance of *concentration* (see pages 61-73) and of *association* (see last section of this chapter).

A group of students were given practice for three hours spread over four weeks in memorizing poems and nonsense syllables without being told what methods to use. Another group practised memorizing poems and nonsense syllables but were instructed in proper methods of memorizing. They were taught the use of attention to meaning (comprehension), active self-testing (recitation), learning by wholes, mental alertness (concentration), confidence in one's ability (autosuggestion), and associations (see pages 98-107). When both groups were given a memory test the group which had used the above methods averaged 30-40 per cent better results than the other. [72]

Are we entitled to assume, as we do in this book, that conclusions reached as a result of experiments conducted in the psychological laboratory are valid when applied to the practical problems of everyday life? This problem itself formed the subject of an experimental investigation carried out in the field of learning by the Russian psychologist D. B. Elkonin.

Elkonin studied an experimental class in which the programme and methods of instruction in the pupil's mother tongue and in arithmetic had been altered in accordance with recommendations based on the findings of experimental research. He found that the amount of time spent in learning the material was reduced and that the quality of the learning was improved. [73]

3. Avoiding Interference

We now come to the third reason why memories are lost, i.e., through interference from other memories. The practical task that faces us is to discover how such interference can be eliminated or cut down to a minimum.

For a few minutes after a memory trace is formed it is easily disturbed. If left undisturbed the trace hardens or consolidates and can resist interference from other memory traces. During the process of consolidation, however, it is still subject to a type of interference known as retroactive inhibition from later memory traces.

The principle of retroactive inhibition states that the memory trace of an earlier activity is impaired by that of a later one.

In other words, we tend to forget a certain thing not simply because it is a week ago since we learned it, but because we have since learned other things, the memory traces of which have interfered with the memory trace of the original thing.

The problem of memory efficiency, then, is the problem of reducing this interference to a minimum in order to give the memory trace the chance to set or consolidate. The brain begins to forget part of what it has learned almost immediately after learning it. Much of the forgetting occurs during the first fifteen minutes, and is due to the facts being crowded out by new experiences. This means that we must allow something we have learned to set or consolidate in our minds if we are to remember it.

There are several ways in which this can be done.

The most favourable conditions of remembering would occur if no activity at all followed the learning of the material until it had had a chance to become consolidated. The practical application of this principle has been shown by the discovery that if memorizing is followed by sleep, the memorized material is retained better than if further waking activity ensues.

We forget less rapidly during sleep than during waking hours. While we are asleep we do not learn other things likely to interfere with the memory of what we have already learned. This fact argues in favour of learning periods being followed by sleep. When we study in the evening we should go to bed afterwards rather than take up further waking activity. This not only helps us to assimilate work already done, but also refreshes us for the work of the following day.

The lesson may be revised in the morning before the activity of the day makes us forget a great deal of it. The process of forgetting is thus delayed not only by the period of sleep but also by the subsequent revision.

Jenkins and Dallenbach have made a special study of this problem. They showed that if subjects retire and sleep immediately after learning, retention after twenty-four hours is better than it is if they remain awake for a few hours after learning. They had their subjects learn certain materials and tested them after one or two or four or eight hours. During these intervals the subjects either slept or were occupied with their normal day's business. The results were invariably superior when the subjects had been sleeping than they were after an equal interval of daytime activities. [74]

Johnson and Swan, too, found that work done just before sleep was 6.5 per cent superior to that performed immediately on waking. [75]

During sound sleep there is, in spite of occasional dreams, probably a minimum of mental activity. Thus we can see why retention is much better during sleep than it is during waking.

Even if we do not sleep after learning, a period of rest or relaxation helps us to remember. If you cannot adopt the above procedure and go to bed after studying, avoid doing any other mental work, especially of a similar kind, before retiring to bed. A few minutes of 'taking it easy' directly after learning a lesson make for better remembering than an equal period devoted to strenuous mental activity.

If you must memorize something for use within a short time, try to arrange matters so that the briefest possible period elapses between the time of memorizing and the time of recalling. Then the interfering impressions will be as few as possible.

Further strenuous mental occupation, especially of a similar nature, is unfavourable to remembering. The more active we are in the interval, the more likely we are to forget. The greatest loss of retention occurs by shifting directly to material of a very similar kind. However, the better we learn the original task, the more likely we are to remember it even in spite of what we do afterwards.

The greatest loss of retention occurs by shifting directly from one lesson to another of a very similar kind. Therefore the student should see that even if he must engage in further mental activity after learning, it is of as different a kind as possible. If one period of study must be followed immediately by another, arrange to switch to that form of learning which is least similar to the one in which you have just been engaged.

For example, do not follow one branch of mathematics with another, but arithmetic or algebra might very well be followed by a foreign language. After studying psychology one should not turn directly to philosophy but rather to mathematics or chemistry.

There is another way in which mental processes are inhibited, causing us to forget. This is known as the principle of proactive inhibition, which states that mental activity that precedes learning also prevents us from remembering what we have learned. We forget something that we have learned because we have learned other things before. Not merely are old memories obliterated by the new but also new ones by the old.

To illustrate this point with a homely example, we may say that the absent-minded professor leaves his umbrella on the bus not only on account of his wife's reminder to post a letter given to him *after* he picked up his umbrella from the hall-stand, but also on account of the lecture which he prepared the previous night *before* he picked up his umbrella.

Therefore the student would be well advised to see that before commencing to study a lesson he takes a brief rest rather than engaging in other mental activity.

Proactive inhibition also depends on similarity in the same way as does retroactive inhibition. Similarity between the inhibiting and the inhibited processes heightens the degree of the disturbance.

Hence even if you must take up the study of a subject immediately after engaging in some other mental activity, you should endeavour to ensure that it is as different as possible.

All this lends increased plausibility to the theory that forgetting is a matter of disturbing interaction among memory traces rather than of a deterioration which each memory trace undergoes independently. [76], [77]

4. Repression

The fourth cause of forgetting is repression. A memory is forgotten by being repressed or denied admittance into the conscious mind. Having something on the tip of one's tongue indicates that a repression is operating; the harder one tries to remember it the more difficult it becomes.

To remember, then, the repression must be relieved. A repressed memory can be recalled if the repression is undone. There are two ways in which this is accomplished. One is by increasing the strength of the memory itself. How to do this has been explained in the three preceding sections of this chapter. The other is by reducing the strength of the resistance opposed to the repressed memory.

For example, if one turns one's attention to other matters, the resistance may be weakened and the repressed memory will pop up spontaneously into consciousness. This is the basis of the method in which we try to recall something by *relying upon the memory occurring to us spontaneously*. A forgotten name may suddenly spring to mind after we cease to think about it.

A name which is 'on the tip of your tongue' can be remembered by not trying to remember it. This illustrates the operation of the law of reversed effort, which states that in a conflict between will and imagination the latter proves the stronger. You can use this law in a helpful way by trying not to remember the name (will) but at the same time thinking that you will remember it (imagination). In this conflict imagination proves the stronger: the forgotten name springs to mind.

The recall of material that has temporarily escaped our memory can sometimes be achieved by the simple method of *saying the alphabet* slowly to ourselves, pausing after each letter to allow time for the process of association to work. If the forgotten material is framed in words, sooner or later we must come to a letter which is associated with one of those words. The association may lead to the recall of the forgotten material in its entirety. As soon as we utter the letter in question, what we are seeking to remember may occur to us. For example, a housewife said: 'I remembered a name by going through the letters of the alphabet.'

A man said: 'I have quite a number of photographs of my wartime army comrades mounted in an album. The name of the person is written on the back of the photograph. Having forgotten most of the names, I decided to try a little experiment to remember them. I just thought of the person for a few minutes and then mentally went through the alphabet, and on reaching the initial letter of the wanted name, I found that the name itself followed. When a name came to mind, it proved, on looking at the back of the photograph, to be right. This is the method I have always used for remembering names and have found it very successful.'

This method can be adapted to recalling foreign language equivalents of English words. The English word should be held in mind and the foreign alphabet worked through until the equivalent is remembered.

It can also serve if the material is in algebraic form, e.g. an algebraic equation. If the material is wholly in numerical form, try *saying numbers to yourself,* starting with 0. In this way you may be able to recall forgotten telephone numbers, house numbers, dates, sums of money, football and cricket scores, etc.

The resistance to a repressed memory also becomes weaker in sleep, so that during a dream we may recall something which has been repressed in waking life. Therefore the memory can be recalled by *interpreting a dream.* This is a problem which the author has dealt with in a previous book to which the reader is referred for further information.*

Sometimes we can recall something forgotten by *being reminded of it through something said or done* during the course of the day. For example, a lady said: 'If I cannot remember a name or address, I leave it at the back of my mind for an hour or so and continue with my work; then quite suddenly something will happen to remind me of it.'

Another method useful for recalling memory material is 'sleeping on it'. This is described as follows by a person who tried it. 'I have my own system,' she said, 'for recalling forgotten material. On retiring I tell myself silently that I shall recall what I want to know, and then I promptly go to sleep. I wake up in the morning nearly always knowing the answer to my problem.'

(a) *The Solution of Problems in Sleep*

Another instance is that of a university student who said: 'Whilst asleep I solved a mathematical problem which had defeated me when awake. Every weekend I have mathematical problems to work out. I am in the habit of working on them on Saturday evenings. One evening, however, I couldn't fathom a certain problem. Nor could I do so on Sunday, but went to bed on Sunday night and worked it out in a dream. On Monday I found that I was the only one who had been able to solve it out of a class of over fifty.'

Inspiration often comes in this way. For example, a schoolboy would

Dreams: Their Mysteries Revealed (Aquarian Press, 1969).

go to sleep with problems still unsolved. As he awoke in the morning the answers were quickly obtained.

In *From the Workshop of Discoveries,* O. Loewi writes as follows: [78]

> In the night of Easter Saturday, 1921, I awoke, turned on the light, and jotted down a few notes on a tiny slip of paper. Then I fell asleep again. It occurred to me at six o'clock in the morning that during the night I had written down something most important, but I was unable to decipher the scrawl. That Sunday was the most desperate day in my whole scientific life. During the next night, however, I awoke again, at three o'clock, and I remembered what it was.
>
> This time I did not take any risk; I got up immediately, went to the laboratory, made the experiment on the frog's heart . . . and at five o'clock, the chemical transmission of nervous impulse was conclusively proved.

Sometimes one comes across a case in which a person seems to remember something which he has never experienced. In a way inspiration itself is rather like this. Nevertheless, such an explanation is probably more apparent than real. Here is an instance in which a person recalled something he had no recollection of ever having experienced.

A doctor said that he once heard an elderly patient who was delirious speaking fluent French, although normally the patient knew nothing of the language. Let us assume that the patient had served in France in World War I. The French he would hear would be recorded in an odd corner of his unconscious mind, from which it might well emerge in delirium. Perhaps the patient was not in France in World War I? Very well, then — he had been to France since? He had heard French people speaking in this country? He had seen a French film? Any one of a number of possibilities might account for his knowledge of that language. Somehow or other the man must have come into contact with spoken French, and this experience lay at the root of his behaviour in delirium.

Reintegration (see pages 82-83) can also be used as a method of recalling something which has been temporarily repressed or forgotten. This is illustrated by the following experiences reported by Miss C. L.:

'As a child at school and on other occasions I was often told, when asked a question, "You won't find the answer on the ceiling!" But the point was that I *did.* For example, I would be asked, "What was the date of the Battle of Hastings?'' If I was in the same room I had only to look at the same object which I had been watching when told the date. Then it would come back to my mind in a flash.'

The forgotten memory may be recalled even if the attendant circumstances are only reinstated in imagination instead of in reality. As the above person put it:

'If I was in another room I would use the ceiling to project a mental picture of the scene where I learned the date, and then the answer would be there. I still do this, especially with music. For example, I can recall the title of a tune which is running through my head by thinking of the instrument on which I first heard it played.'

'Some years ago,' she went on, 'I used to work in a neighbourhood where there are a number of small streets whose names I didn't know. I always managed not to lose myself until one evening on my way home from work I stopped and realized I must have taken a wrong turning somewhere. I found my way by going back to a spot I remembered and starting off again from there.'

She hoped that reinstating the original conditions under which she learned the route would enable her to recall the memory of it.

Therefore, if you are trying to bring something back to mind, *repeat or imagine yourself repeating the situation in which you originally experienced it.*

(b) *Free Association*
Usually, however, a special technique is required to relieve a repression. The best method of weakening the resistance is, in fact, the method known as 'free association'.

Free association has been described by Freud as putting oneself 'into a condition of calm self-observation, without trying to think of anything, and then to communicate everything which he becomes inwardly aware of, feelings, thoughts, remembrances, in the order in which they arise in his mind.' A person doing this should avoid any inclination 'to select from or to exclude any of the ideas (associations), whether because they are too "disagreeable," or too "indiscreet" to be mentioned, or too "unimportant" or "irrelevant" or "nonsensical" to be worth saying . . . he has only to attend to what is on the surface consciously in his mind, and to abandon all objections to whatever he finds, no matter what form they take.'[79]

To make practical use of this method get a pencil and a writing pad;

retire to some quiet place; think of something connected with what you want to recall, and ask yourself: 'What do I remember next?' Write down whatever comes to mind. Then ask yourself again: 'What do I remember next?' Again write the answer. Proceed thus until you recall the desired memory or until you have had enough and put the method aside for the next sitting.

A simple example of a chain of associations that resulted in the recall of a forgotten name is given by Freud in his *Introductory Lectures on Psycho-Analysis* (p.92). He found that he could not remember the name of the small country on the Riviera of which Monte Carlo is the capital. 'I delved into all my knowledge about the country; I thought of Prince Albert . . . of his marriages, of his passion for deep-sea exploration — in fact of everything I could summon up, but all to no purpose. So I gave up trying . . . and, instead . . . let substitute names come into my mind . . .; Monte Carlo . . . Piedmont, Albania, Montevideo, Colico . . . Montenegro . . . Then I noticed that four of the substitute names have the same syllable 'mon,' and immediately I recalled the forgotten word . . . "Monaco".'[80]

He adds the reason that led him to forget the name for the time being: 'Monaco is the Italian name for Munich, and it was some thoughts connected with this town which had acted as an inhibition.' This illustrates the third or fourth of the causes of forgetting mentioned on page 46, i.e. interference from other impressions or the repression of an unpleasant memory.

Another example will be found in Theodor Reik's *The Inner Experience of a Psycho-Analyst,* where the author tells how by means of free association of ideas he remembered the poem in which occur the lines, 'for when true love awakens, dies The Self, that despot, dark and vain.'[81]

Use of the above method has evoked some encouraging reports from persons who have tried it. For example, one of them said: 'I have tried the free association of ideas exercise with great success. It usually takes only about five or ten minutes to recall a name, which in some instances arrives suddenly "out of the blue" after a relaxation of effort.'

Another reports: 'I have practised the memory exercise of free association of ideas, and find that I really can remember names and data from years previous.'

'I thought about the person whose name I wished to recall and as many things about him as I could remember,' said a woman, 'and I was then able to recall the name.'

Recently the writer was unable to remember the address of a relative who lived in a town in Hertfordshire. He applied the simple method prescribed above. Writing down all the ideas that the name of the town reminded him of, he very soon arrived at the address he was seeking.

'It worked, taking about twenty minutes,' said a man. 'I started with a crotchet sign used in music, went on to "tune", then "Tunley", and finally "Nunley", which was the name I wanted.'

'I tried it,' said a Nigerian student, 'and remembered a name which in my language is the word for rolling a piece of wood on the ground. It is "Abiri". In calling the name to mind I saw a mental image of a man rolling a piece of wood on the floor.'

A young woman said: 'I tried to remember the name of my German teacher at school. Amongst other things, woods, trees and flowers kept cropping up. The German for tree is Baum and the teacher's name was Baumgarten.'

'There were huge gaps in my memory,' stated a man. 'I have relived several past experiences and have gone back in memory through a great part of my childhood days by means of free association of ideas. My memory is now complete.' This result was achieved in less than five months.

'I have been doing the free association of ideas,' said Mr N. V., 'and I now realize how the unconscious mind speaks in a language of symbols. On trying to remember the name of a friend whom I knew in the Services, I ended with a mental picture of a park with lots of sun. The chap's name is Parkinson.'

The author wanted to recall the name of a man with whom he had had some dealings. He remembered that the man lived in Wales. He therefore sat down and asked himself: 'What does Wales remind me of?' He wrote down the name 'Mason'. Then he asked himself: 'What does Mason remind me of?' He wrote 'home'. He continued to practise this simple method for a few minutes, writing down the following chain of associated names: Jones — Carless — Curtis — Clapham — King — Royal — Roy — Ray — Raines — Real — Simpson — Smart — Trevor — Cannon — Walters. The next name that came was recognized as the one sought: Williams.

A student said: 'I tried free association of ideas for remembering the meaning of the French word *coudrier*. I didn't go on very long before

I got as far as ''willow tree''. Then I thought of ''green''. I connected ''green'' with ''hazel twigs'', so I got it in the end. *Coudrier* means ''hazel tree''.'

'I find,' said Mrs R. D., 'that I have been using very much the same method as this for calling things to mind all my life. I tried the experiment with the story of *Jane Eyre*, which I read at ten years of age. It was possible to recall the whole story.'

Mr L. E. said: 'I tried to recall the name of my maths master at school. I thought of old school pals, escapades, dreams and hopes, school exercises. Whilst browsing among these memories of the past, I recalled being given a lift in his car. Then I remembered his name: Mr. Carson!'

(c) *Laws of Association*

The principle of association is invaluable not only in relieving repressions, but also in memorizing the material we wish to retain.

For example, do you have difficulty in remembering whether to write *separate* or *seperate*? To separate means to part. Associate *separate* with *part*, and you will easily remember the spelling.

In church you go up for communion to the altar rail and it is important that on your return you should find the right pew. Since they all look alike how are you to do it? You can associate the position of your pew with something else, e.g. you can remind yourself that it is three rows behind the churchwarden's pew, or that it is level with the third column from the foot of the chancel steps, etc.

According to the press, a security firm who provide a bandit-proof safe rely upon the principle of association. They arrange that only the proprietor of the safe shall know the combination which opens it, and they instruct him to remember it by associating it with something personal to himself, such as a birthday, wedding anniversary, etc.

Association of ideas is a basic fact of mental life which has been known since the days of Aristotle. It accounts for the way in which one idea occurs after another. For example, on the day when a woman was moving out of a house, she had a mental 'flashback' to the day, twenty-one years before, when she had moved into it. The 'flashback' occurred because the present experience was associated with the earlier one.

Another illustration is given by a teacher who said: 'During my training I learned, in teaching something new, to tag it on to something the children already knew.'

There are three laws of association (similarity, contrast, contiguity). The law of association by similarity states that two ideas may be associated if they resemble each other. For example, trying to remember a name, a man thought of a pigeon, then of a pouter pigeon. Then the name came to him: Poulter. It was associated with 'pouter' by similarity.

In another instance the name Ede, which a man had been trying to recall for several days, was associated by similarity with Sir Anthony Eden. The name flashed across his mind when he picked up an evening newspaper and started to read an article about the former Prime Minister.

A third case which illustrates the law of association by similarity is the following. A woman reported: 'I tried to remember a name. I had a session of writing down my memories, but without result. Then I left it, but, on thinking about it afterwards, this thought came into my mind, "What a *hue* and cry all over a name!" The missing name was *Hughes*.'

The law of association by contrast states that two ideas may be associated if they contrast with each other. For example, someone mentions the word 'day'. We at once think of the word 'night'.

The law of association by contiguity states that two ideas may be associated if they have occurred together. For example, a well-known song has the line: 'Moonlight and roses bring memories of you'. Moonlight and roses were associated by contiguity with the song writer's beloved because they had probably all been present together on the same occasion.

Vergilius Ferm in an article on 'Memorizing' in *A Dictionary of Pastoral Psychology* says that he remembers 1859 as the date of the publication of Darwin's *Origin of Species* because he associates it with the year preceding the founding of his alma mater in 1860. [82] This, too, illustrates the law of association by contiguity.

Another illustration is provided by a man who said: 'On holiday some years ago I met a man who was a home decorator by trade. We became good friends and he offered to decorate my home very cheaply at any time. When I wanted to take advantage of his services, I was unfortunately unable to remember his name. I wrote down all I remembered about his appearance and character, but with no success. But at a second sitting, while trying to recall any other ideas associated with him, I thought of the fact that he was willing to do a *job* for my family; then I recalled his name. It was *Work*.'

Ideas are more likely to be associated the more frequently, recently and vividly they have occurred together. The laws of frequency (or repetition), recency and vividness (or intensity) are known as the secondary laws of association, in contrast to the ones already mentioned, which are known as the primary laws of association.

The law of frequency states that two things are more likely to be associated the more frequently they have occurred together. Frequently performed acts, habits or responses tend to be learned better than those infrequently practised. For example, a student said: 'The more I study my lesson the more I understand it.' Reliance upon the drill method of instruction exemplifies the use of this principle of learning, which emphasizes the number of repetitions employed during learning.

The law of recency states that two things are more likely to be associated the more recently they have occurred together. For example, it is a common experience to find that the dreams we remember deal with the events of the day before.

Suppose two sides of an argument, for example in a debate, are presented to an audience in succession. Which will be remembered better — the one presented first or the one presented last? Is it better to 'get your oar in first' or to 'have the last word'?

This question has been settled by an experimental study in which the subjects listened to recorded broadcasts of news items. The items were presented in a different order to each of twelve groups of subjects. After hearing the broadcasts the subjects were tested to find out which items they remembered best.

It was found that the items in the second half of the broadcast were remembered better than those in the first half. The conclusion we are entitled to draw is that from the point of view of memory it is better to have the last say. [83]

The law of intensity or vividness states that two things are more likely to be associated the more vividly they have occurred together. This principle holds that the more vivid an impression is, the better it is retained.

For example, a housewife stated: 'The dreams that I remember for a long time afterwards are much more distinct than the ones I remember only for the next morning.' Or, as Mr E. P. C. put it: 'My recollections of a dream are dependent upon the vividness of the dream.'

The law of frequency raises an interesting problem. This is the question of whether repetition in itself is sufficient to ensure that something is learnt or that a skill is acquired. The common belief that it is is enshrined in the popular saying that 'Practice makes perfect'. How far is this supported by modern psychological theory? If I work at a subject long enough, can I be sure that in time I shall master it?

Discussing this question, a writer remarks, 'Mere frequency of repetition is now known to play only a minor part in learning. Effective motivation is necessary for learning to take place. An enormous number of repetitions made passively without the intention to learn are proved to be ineffective compared with a much smaller number made with effort to retain the learned material.'

Another writer quotes the case of the subject of an experiment in a psychological laboratory who was supposed to memorize a list of nonsense syllables. After the list had been passed before him many times without his giving the signal that he was ready to recite, the experimenter remarked that he seemed to be having trouble in memorizing the syllables. 'Oh! I didn't understand that I was to learn them,' he said, and it was found that he had made almost no progress. The will to learn, in fact, was absent.

In another experiment the subjects tried to draw three-inch lines while blindfolded. They practised drawing hundreds of lines, but were not told how well they were doing. As a result they showed no improvement. As soon as the psychologist began to say, 'Right,' when they succeeded, the subjects began to improve. This experiment illustrates that mere repetition by itself does not ensure that a skill is acquired. [84]

Psychology thus proves the fallacy of the popular axiom that 'Practice makes perfect' by showing that incessant practice without effective motivation or the intention to learn does not make perfect. Without a strong reason for doing an act, it merely makes a moderate level of skill more automatic. Motivation is an important factor in learning and acquiring a skill.

To the above three main laws of association the American psychologist Thorndike added a fourth, which is known as the law of assimilation or the principle of generalization. This states that a person may react towards a whole situation as he has reacted towards some part of it or towards the whole or part of some other situation like it.

This is illustrated by the curious phenomenon of memory called *déjà vu*, to which reference has already been made in Chapter 2 (see page 52). The explanation we advanced there was that the present situation seems familiar because it resembles in part or in whole some situation in the past which we have now forgotten. We react with the feeling that 'we have been here before' towards the situation because we have already reacted in that way towards some part of it or towards some situation like it.

Again, a person may react towards all of a group of people as he has reacted towards some or one of them. Someone who has repeatedly experienced defeat or failure in one situation or a few may come to experience feelings of inferiority in a large number of situations. As the proverb puts it, 'Once bitten, twice shy.'

For example, a girl said: 'In my childhood, if my mother took offence at something I had chanced to say, she would not speak to me for days or even weeks on end. Now I am afraid to say anything to other people in case I should offend them.' She was reacting to other people as she had learned to react to one person in her childhood.

By association, then, is meant the tendency to link impressions with other impressions already in the mind or acquired at the same time or place. Everyone appreciates the value of association as a means of recalling faces and events of the past which have been apparently quite obliterated. Every idea that we have is associated with other ideas, and by following back the lines of association a distinct image can be reproduced.

We should *take advantage of all rational associations of ideas* to improve our memorizing. The more impressions there are associated with the thing to be remembered, the readier and more certain is its recollection. It is as if there are several paths converging into one. It is only necessary to find any one of these paths and follow it to reach the desired goal. The obvious conclusion is that the greater the stock of knowledge possessed by a mind the easier it is for that stock to be augmented.

(d) *How to Use Association*

Suppose your wife gives you a letter to post. What can you do to ensure that you remember to post it? The answer is: associate the letter with the idea of the first letter-box you see. Then when you actually see the letter-box, you will recall the need to post the letter. The sight of the letter-box will bring the letter to your mind.

Again, a resemblance between an incident in history and a current event may form an association that will enable the event in history to be easily recalled.

In the learning of foreign language words the principle of association is especially useful.

Two Russian psychologists conducted an experiment in which German words new to the secondary school pupils being tested were translated without explanation. This method was compared with that in which the translation was accompanied by an etymological explanation of the word's meaning. They found, as might be expected, that words memorized by the second method were retained better and longer than the 'one-word' translation method. [85] The reason is that the second method has two great advantages:

1. It enables the learner to form stable associations between words he already knows in his own or the foreign language and the new word he wishes to learn.
2. Working out the etymological connections is a more active method. It makes the pupils think more, demanding more of them and stimulating their intellectual activity better than the passive method of committing to memory the German word and its meaning.

Let us take a simple example to illustrate this point. Suppose you want to learn the German equivalent for 'boy'. To do this by the first method would mean that you study the following one-word translation:

der Knabe — boy

To present vocabulary in this form is the method adopted almost uniformly in language textbooks. Can we wonder that language teaching rarely achieves the results that are expected of it?

Let us compare this method with the second method, in which the one-word translation is supplemented by an etymological explanation. The material to be learned might then be presented as follows:

der Knabe — boy (The German word *Knabe* is cognate with the English word 'knave', which originally meant 'boy' but now has a pejorative sense.)

The inclusion of this explanation means that between *der Knabe* and 'boy' we insert an associative link which makes remembering easier. In reality the way we are now presenting the material is like this:

$$der\ Knabe - \frac{associative\ link}{(knave)} - boy$$

Furthermore, by setting ourselves the task of digging out this piece of etymological information we have played a more active part in memorization than is required by the simple act of trying to learn the one-word equivalent. *To take a more active part in learning is a help in remembering the material better.*

All learning is, in fact, governed by this fundamental principle of associating one thing with another. You can make use of it by discovering the relations between the various parts of what you are studying and by linking up what you learn with what you know already.

For example, in the army a recruit is taught to remember fire orders by associating them with the letters of the word D R I N K. Thus he is taught to associate D with Designation, R with Range, I with Indication, N with Number of rounds, and K with Kind of fire.

An example of the use of association with the intention of supporting memory occurs in a passage by the Roman historian Tacitus. He is describing the intervention of the Romans in a dispute between Cartimandua, queen of the Celtic tribe of the Brigantes, and her estranged husband Venutius. He tells how Cartimandua captured members of Venutius' family, whereupon Venutius invaded the kingdom. The Romans went to the aid of the queen, first with some cohorts, then with a legion. All this happened over a period of time, but the historian, perceiving in it cause and effect, associates the occurrences with each other as though they were contiguous in time. 'These events,' he writes, 'though occurring under two governors and occupying several years, I have closely connected lest, if related separately, they might be less easily remembered.'

Another familiar example is the rhyme that associates the months with the number of days in each. We are able to remember how many days each month has by recalling 'Thirty days hath September, April, June and November . . .'

A child learning the piano is taught to remember the names of the notes in the spaces of the treble clef by associating them with each other in the word F A C E. Similarly, the notes on the lines in the treble clef are remembered by associating them with the initial letters of the words in the sentence '*Every Good Boy Deserves Fun*'.

The present writer, who had studied Latin before he took up German, remembers the order of adverbs in a German sentence by associating the initial letters of Time, Mode and Place with their order in the Latin word T E M P U S.

A useful mnemonic for remembering the seven deadly sins is P E L A G A S — Pride, Envy, Lust, Anger, Gluttony, Avarice, Sloth.

A more elaborate one for remembering the names of English counties is: 'Three Boys and three Men of Leeds and Northern Civil Defence Headquarters Were OKAY When Taking GCE in seven Subjects.' This sentence gives all forty-five counties of England. It works out as follows:

* Three B(oys): Bedfordshire (1), Berkshire (2), Buckinghamshire (3).
* Three M(en): Greater Manchester (4), Merseyside (5), West Midlands (6).

The word 'quarters' in 'Headquarters' gives you a clue that for each of the letters L, N, C, D, and H there are four counties:

* L(eeds): Lancashire (7), Leicestershire (8), Lincolnshire (9), Greater London (10).
* N(orthern): Norfolk (11), Northamptonshire (12), Northumberland (13), Nottinghamshire (14).
* C(ivil): Cambridgeshire (15), Cheshire (16), Cornwall (17), Cumbria (18).
* D(efence): Derbyshire (19), Devon (20), Dorset (21), Durham (22).
* H(eadquarters): Hampshire (23), Hereford & Worcester (24), Hertfordshire (25), Humberside (26).

The words 'W(ere) OKAY W(hen) T(aking)' give us nine more: Warwickshire (27), Oxfordshire (28), Kent (29), Avon (30), (North, South, West) Yorkshire (31, 32, 33), Wiltshire (34), Tyne & Wear (35). From GCE we get: Gloucestershire (36), Cleveland (37), Essex (38).
    And the remaining seven are given by:
* Seven S(ubjects): Shropshire (39), Somerset (40), Staffordshire (41), Suffolk (42), Surrey (43), East Sussex (44), West Sussex (45).

(e) *How to Remember a Speech*

A man had to propose a toast to the bridegroom's parents at his daughter's wedding reception. He wanted to know how he could remember his speech.

The speech was as follows:

Ladies and Gentlemen, —

In proposing this toast I must ask you to overlook my inexperience as a public speaker. I hope that what I have to say will atone for any shortcomings in the way I say it.

I would like to take this opportunity of thanking Mr and Mrs Smith for the son they have given my wife and me, and I hope that they will think that the daughter we have been happy to give them is a fair 'swop'. I would like to improve upon the old maxim that 'a trouble shared is a troubled halved' by saying that a happiness shared is a happiness doubled.

David's parents may well be proud of their son today, for they see him taking the first step on a new and rewarding path. That this step is being taken in company with our daughter is a cause of rejoicing and thankfulness to my wife and myself.

We all hope that the lucky couple will be inspired by the example of harmony that they see in the marriage of Mr and Mrs Smith. I am sure that you all share with me the hope that the latter, too, will be able to look back on this day as one of the happiest in *their* lives.

It was not my intention to make a long speech, and already I am overrunning the time I allowed myself. Let me conclude, then, by asking you to rise and drink the health of Mr and Mrs Smith.

The man who was to propose the above toast said: 'I have always had a shocking memory for anything learned by heart. At school I was never able to remember anything, even though I had tried very hard and had spent a long time over it. Sometimes, after a great deal of effort, I can memorize a short piece, but when I have to speak it before other people it runs out of my brain like water through a sieve.'

To anyone else with the same difficulty we offer the same suggestion as to this man. If you want to remember a speech, the thing to do is to make use of a mnemonic. As we have seen, this is a device employing the principle of association. In the case of a speech it is a key word which we can associate with the contents of the speech. All you have to do is to remember the key word, which will remind you of what you want to say.

The above speech consists of five paragraphs, which can be remembered with the help of the mnemonic word UTTER. Each letter of this word gives a clue to the contents of one paragraph. For example, the first paragraph deals with the speaker being *unused* (U) to public speaking; the second paragraph is an expression of *thanks* (T); the third paragraph deals with *taking* a step *together* (T); the fourth paragraph refers to the *example* (E) set by the bridegroom's parents; and the fifth paragraph is a *request* to the company to *rise* (R).

By means of this simple application of the principle of association the whole speech can be committed to memory.

Here is another example of the use of association in remembering. Do you have trouble remembering how to alter your clock when British Summer Time begins and ends? Do you put it forward in spring and back in autumn, or back in spring and forward in autumn? The correct method can be remembered by associating it with two little phrases with which you are already familiar: 'Spring forward — fall back.' The word 'fall,' of course, means 'autumn'.

Students in teachers' training colleges are taught that an essential stage in preparing their lessons is to ask themselves what the pupils already know about the subject they intend to teach. This is so that they can build on sure foundations, associating the new with the old. It is yet another illustration of the value of association in training the memory.

Now let us summarize what we have learned in the form of four practical hints:

1.   Give your full attention to what you wish to remember.
2.   Repeat it until you know it really well.
3.   Make yourself more interested by means of autosuggestion.
4.   Take advantage of associations of ideas.

Attention — Repetition — Interest — Association: these are the keys to a better memory.

4.

Mnemonics for Learning Power

In Chapter 3 we showed how little verbal tricks (which are sometimes in rhyming form) can help you to learn. For instance, we suggested that four points about concentration (Habit, Interest, Relaxation, and Emotion) can be summarized in the word HIRE. We were giving simple examples of *mnemonics*.

At one time it was the fashion among academic psychologists to sneer at the use of mnemonic devices for learning. For example, in 1948 Professors Boring, Langfeld, and Weld wrote in their *Foundations of Psychology*: 'Various memory systems attempt to guarantee close attention by elaborate devices, memory "crutches". If you will spend the same time and effort directly on the material, you will usually be ahead of the game.'[86]

This view has been echoed by writers who popularize the findings of academic psychology. For example, in his *How to Study* Harry Maddox writes: 'There are a number of memory systems, out of which quacks and pseudo-psychologists still make a living, which claim to improve memory. They mostly depend on developing ingenious and artificial associations between otherwise disconnected facts.'

He continues: 'These systems are, however, so artificial that you should be able to do much better by developing real and logical associations yourself. Learning and recall are in fact about 25 per cent better when sensible logical connexions between items are developed than when artificial connexions are made according to some system. The success of any of the commercial "systems" results more from the stimulus that they give to the learner's efforts than from any other cause. Any intelligent person can do better on his own, provided he gives his attention to the task. Usually it is easy to find an intermediate idea or association which will link the two ideas together.'[87]

The above point of view is open to the following criticisms:

1. Artificial associations are the only way of connecting disconnected facts.
2. They are required because the real and logical associations which this author recommends cannot be found.
3. He offers no proof of his assertion that sensible logical connections are 25 per cent better.
4. His opinion is contradictory for he is saying, in effect, that commercial systems are both successful and a failure as a means of memory training.
5. In the same book in which he claims that 'any intelligent person can do better on his own,' this author admits: 'Even the most gifted students can seldom discover unaided the most effective ways of studying.'

The opinion voiced by Boring, Langfeld, and Weld and supported by Maddox is now regarded as out of date. It was expressed before any real effort had been made to submit mnemonics to the test of scientific validation. It represents no more than a personal prejudice voiced in the absence of solid evidence. When academic psychologists persuaded themselves to carry out such research, they had to change their tune. A different attitude prevailed when, after comparing learning with mnemonics and learning without mnemonics, they found that mnemonics were of value after all.

As early as 1960 we find Dr Burton G. Andreas, Associate Professor of Psychology, University of Rochester, USA, admitting in his textbook *Experimental Psychology*: 'In the practical art of remembering, many people rely on mnemonic devices . . . Since mnemonics devices are demonstrably beneficial in certain retention tasks, they must embody certain principles of memory.'[88]

In 1975 Dr Vernon Gregg, lecturer in psychology at Birkbeck College, University of London, wrote in *Human Memory*: 'Most people, with practice, can achieve surprising levels of performance using mnemonic schemes . . . Employment of imaginal coding in mnemonic devices can lead to remarkable levels of remembering, suggesting that the capacity of visual imaginal memory to record episodic phenomena is very great.'[89]

And more recently we even find Dr Alan D. Baddeley chiding his fellow academic psychologists for not giving more attention to mnemonics. In *The Psychology of Memory* he complains: 'Although there has in recent years been an increase in work on mnemonic systems and the question of how memory performance can be improved, this aspect of memory has continued to interest the layman more than the psychologist.'[90]

1. Simple Mnemonics

We have said that memory depends upon association — the linking of one bit of information to another. How do you acquire the habit of establishing these associations? As your memory is like a computer, it needs operating instructions just as a computer does. That is, you must program it.

Simple mnemonics represent one method of programming the human computer. A well-known one is the mnemonic for the colours of the spectrum: Richard of York goes battling in vain (red, orange, yellow, green, blue, indigo, violet). A university professor once told me that in his student days the spectrum was learned in reverse order with the following mnemonic: Virgins in bed give you odd reactions!

Astronomers classify stars by using letters of the alphabet: O, B, A, F, G, K, M, R, N, and S. They remember this classification with the help of the mnemonic: Oh, be a fine girl; kiss me right now — smack (or: sweetheart)!

According to student Mr R.S., a mnemonic found handy in chemistry for remembering the hexose sugars is: All altruists gladly make gum in gallon tanks (allose, altrose, glucose, mannose, gulose, idose, galactose, talose).

Mnemonics can be useful in fields other than formal learning. For example, road safety and electioneering have both seen them pressed into service. The Green Cross code for teaching young children to cross the road safely on their own was based on the mnemonic word SPLINK (Stop at a safe place; on the pavement; look and listen; if traffic is coming, let it pass; when no traffic is near, cross; keep looking and listening while you cross).

The names of political (and other) organizations are often arranged so that the initials of the words composing them form a mnemonic. For example, a by-election candidate campaigned on the slogan 'Make your BID for . . .' BID stood for British Independent Democracy. His campaign watchword was SERVE — a mnemonic summarizing his aims: S for Supra party, E for Energetic Commonwealth, R for Real representation in the Commons, V for Value of the individual, and E for Essential v. non-essential.

A frequently-met criticism was voiced by a student as follows: 'It seems to me that mnemonics provide a sound method of aiding memory but do not improve the quality of natural memory.' What he meant was that, if you use artificial aids, you end up by becoming wholly dependent upon them. This objection sounds as though it might be valid in theory. But in practice it does not in the long run turn out to be the case. Artificial aids can be regarded as merely temporary props, which can be discarded when they have served their purpose of making the material well enough known that it can be remembered without them.

In any case, the regular practice of forming associations, which is the habit encouraged by mnemonics, is ultimately of permanent value in improving the quality of natural memory.

2. Types of Mnemonics
The examples we have given so far illustrate three of several types of simple mnemonic devices. Without claiming that the list is exhaustive, we can classify simple mnemonics into a number of groups:

Initial letters
Kippers hardly dare move during cold months. (Descending order of the metric scale: kilo-, hecto-, deca-, metre, deci-, centi-, milli-.)

God bless you. (Order of balls at bottom end of snooker table: green, brown, yellow.)

You go brown before potting black. (Order in which the balls should be potted: yellow, green, brown, blue, pink, black.)

Meaningful acronyms
HOMES. (Great Lakes of North America: Huron, Ontario, Michigan, Erie, Superior.)

Meaningless acronyms
GIGSEILM. (Branches of psychology: General, Individual, Genetic, Social, Educational, Industrial, Legal, Medical.)

Rhyming jingles
> Right over left, then left over right,
> And you can pull a reef-knot tight.   (Sailing)

> Beer on whisky
> Very risky:
> Whisky on beer
> Never fear.   (Avoiding a hangover)

Associative mnemonics
When a woman has ants in her pants, the mites go up and the tights come down. (Stalagmites and stalactites.)

Digits represented by words containing the same number of letters
I wish I knew the root of two. (1.414 — the square root of 2.)

Play on words
Spring forward, fall back. (British summer time.)

   Where mnemonics codify the material in a shortened form, as, for instance, in the case of acronyms, they are known as *reductive*. On the other hand, where the material is memorized by being enlarged upon, as in the case of rhyming mnemonics, the technique is called *elaborative*.

3. Devise Your Own

It is an interesting and useful exercise to devise your own mnemonics. For instance, the present writer used the mnemonic word FIRE for helping the staff of his firm to learn the fire-drill:

> F ile out of the building.
> I gnore coats and cars.
> R eport across the road.
> E nter again only when safe.

Everyone knows the spelling mnemonic 'I before E except after C'. But because this does not cover all cases, the writer refined it as follows:

> Use I before E
> Except after C;
> When A or I is the sound,
> It's the other way round.

It now takes care of words like: deign, height, forfeit, etc. Even so, there are still exceptions such as: mischief, sieve!

Here is an example applying to the spelling of individual words:

> A rule that's meaningful
> Is called a princip<u>le</u>,
> But headmasters shall
> Be known as princip<u>al</u>;
> You must also give
> This word as adjective.

The distinction between 'practice' (noun) and 'practise' (verb) can be learned with the help of a similar type of mnemonic:

> <u>Practice</u> with a <u>c</u>
> A noun can only be.
> <u>Practise</u> with an <u>s</u>
> Is just a verb, I guess.

The reader might like to experiment for him/herself by working out a rhyming jingle for the difference between a noun and a verb.

Rhyming jingles have been invented to help pupils to remember dates in history:

The Great Fire of London
> In sixteen hundred and sixty-six
> London burned like rotten sticks.

The Norman Conquest
> William the Conqueror, ten sixty-six,
> Played on the Saxons oft cruel tricks.

Discovery of America
> Columbus sailed the ocean blue
> In fourteen hundred and ninety-two.

Defeat of the Spanish Armada
> The Spanish Armada met its fate
> In fifteen hundred and eighty-eight.

4. Learning the Morse Code

A special problem may call for a special solution involving a mnemonic peculiar to that problem. The following learning task supplies an example of this.

In the Morse code E, a vowel, is represented by a dot and T, a consonant, by a dash.

So if we represent a dot by a vowel and a dash by a consonant, we can devise mnemonic words for those vowels which begin with a dot and those consonants which begin with a dash. They are:

A	.—	AD	(short for 'advertisement')
I	..	IO	(a princess in Greek mythology)
U	..—	UIT	(Dutch for 'out')
B	—...	BEAU	
C	—.—.	COCO	
D	—..	DOE	
G	——.	GRO	(as in 'Gro-Bag')
K	—.—	KEG	
M	——	M.M.	(Military Medal)
N	—.	NO	
Q	——.—	QSOs	(quasi-stellar objects)
X	—..—	—XION	(suffix as in 'inflexion')
Y	—.——	YELL	
Z	——..	ZWEI	(German for 'two')

The vowel O begins with a dash (—). For this we can use the mnemonic word TOM since O is represented by one dash (T) followed by two dashes (M).

This leaves only those consonants which begin with a dot. Obviously for these we cannot use mnemonic words which begin with a vowel. But we can use words which begin with a consonant and in which each vowel represents a dot and each consonant (except the first) a dash.

F	..—.	FAUNA	
H	....	HOOEY	
J	.———	JERKS	
L	.—..	LUCIA	
P	.——.	PIZZA	
R	.—.	RARE	
S	...	SUEY	(as in 'chop-suey')
V	...—	VIEUX	(French for 'old')
W	.——	WELL	

Mnemonics can also be applied to the rules for games.

For example, in backgammon each player has *two* of his stones on his opponent's ace point. The ace point is in the inner table, and the word IN has *two* letters. He has *three* of his stones on his own 8 point. The 8 point is in the outer table, and the word OUT has *three* letters. The positions of the remaining ten stones are easy to remember because they are distributed equally between the player's own 6 point and his opponent's 12 point.

Again, a normal win, where the loser has begun to bear off, scores 1 point. (The word 'win' has one syllable.) A gammon, where the loser has not yet begun to bear off, scores 2 points. (The word 'gammon' has two syllables.) And for the 3 points awarded for a backgammon, where the loser has not begun to bear off and has stones in his opponent's inner table or on the bar, the three syllables in the word 'backgammon' serve as a reminder.

For doubling and redoubling this game provides its own memory aid in the form of the doubling cube.

The game of Mah Jong imposes something of a burden on the memory both in learning and in playing it. Mah Jong is distinguished for its elaborate preliminaries, which include building the Great Wall of China, and its even more elaborate scoring system. The preliminaries require East to remember how to deal. They are best learned by taking one's turn to act as dealer. The scoring system is perhaps the most difficult aspect as far as the memory is concerned. However, it can be rationalized by noting that the points are of four kinds: set points (for Pungs and Kongs); extra or bonus points (e.g., for a pair of dragons); multipliers (usually doubles, e.g., for a Pung or Kong of dragons); and limit hands (scoring 500).

In the first three kinds, the memory is assisted by noting the influence of 2. For example, concealed Pungs and Kongs score twice the value of exposed ones, and a Pung or Kong of major or honour tiles has twice the value of one of minor tiles. Extra points are also 2 for a pair of the prevailing wind, Mah Jong with a tile drawn from the wall, etc.

A little experience in scoring will soon make a player familiar with these combinations.

Some limit hands are probably rare enough not to be worth memorizing. Examples are Scratching a Carrying Pole (Mah Jong by robbing a Kong of the 2 of bamboos) and Moon from the Bottom of the Sea (Mah Jong with 1 of circles as last tile of wall or last discard).

But a few of the commoner ones, where the names can be pressed into service as mnemonics, are:

1. 1-9 of one suit with one of each Wind and any tile paired. (Imagine the 1-9 as the body of a snake, the Winds as its head, and the odd tile as its tongue. The hand is, in fact, called The Snake.)
2. Bamboos and green Dragons only. (The name of this hand provides a simple mnemonic as it is called All Green.)
3. 4 Pungs and a pair. (Think of the Pungs as triplets and the pair as parents. The hand is called Four Concealed Triplets.)
4. 7 pairs of major and/or honour tiles. (Think of the pairs as twins. The hand is called the Heavenly Twins.)
5. Mah Jong with a hand drawn entirely from the wall. (As all the tiles are concealed, it is easy to remember such a hand from its name, which is Hidden Treasure.)

The above examples, taken from a variety of fields, will serve to illustrate the possibilities of applying simple mnemonics to different kinds of materials.

5. Place Memory

In *Experimental Psychology* Dr Burton G. Andreas writes: 'After proceeding around the room having students each name an object, it is then possible to recite the list back in correct order . . . each object being associated with one of the cardinal numbers in sequence. To do this by rote memory in just one hearing is not easy, but a mnemonic device makes it possible. The "memory expert" has prememorized a series of associations . . . With these objects firmly in mind, I need only to associate each named object with the prememorized object. This is done by bringing them together in a visual image, the more bizarre the better . . . Twenty such visualizations are easier to retain than an equal number of pairs associated by rote.'[91]

The method described by Dr Andreas is a fairly modern development of the very much older mnemonic system of *place memory*. This is, in fact, probably the oldest memory system known to man. Place memory was a common method of memorizing at a time when paper on which to make notes was scarce and expensive. Paper replaced the even more costly parchment, but it did not become cheap and plentiful before the fourteenth century. Consequently the medieval student was forced to commit his material to memory rather than to writing. And medieval writers often arranged their material in a way which would permit the use of the place-memory method of learning it.

For example, at Salerno, near Naples, there was a school of medicine famous throughout Europe. In the twelfth century it formalized all it knew in a set of 2,500 precepts called the *Rule of Health*. This work was the basis of all medical teaching in Europe for four hundred years. The medieval physician would commit its precepts to memory by associating each with one of 2,500 places or loci.

It must have been difficult at times to find a series of related loci large enough to accommodate a considerable body of material. Fortunately, in former times knowledge was limited and not open-ended as it is now. The teaching of a subject hardly changed for centuries. A striking example of this is the theorems of Euclid. Devised in about 300 BC, they remained the basis of the teaching of geometry in schools until the recent advent of the New Mathematics.

A small room might provide a couple of dozen loci, a large one perhaps a hundred. More would be found in a large school or church, a monastery, or cathedral. But even so the medieval student of the *Rule of Health* must have been hard put to it to find his 2,500th locus. One supposes that those who succeeded became better doctors than those who didn't.

Place memory is first heard of in connection with the ancient Greek Simonides. Invited to a banquet, he had left the banqueting hall temporarily when the roof collapsed, killing all the guests. Simonides was able to identify the dead through having associated each person with the place which he had occupied.

Metrodorus of Scepsis (106-43 BC) devised a system of place memory based on astrology. He divided the zodiac into 36 decans, each covering ten degrees and each having an associated symbol for mnemonic purposes. Being arranged in numerical order, his places were thus well suited to performing learning tasks.

Among the medieval scholars who used memory systems of this kind, applying them to a series of images of their own choice, were St Thomas Aquinas, Albertus Magnus, Ramon Lull, and others.

The use of rectilinear buildings for this purpose is known as the square art of memory (*ars quadrata*). Giordano Bruno (1548-1600) favoured the round art (*ars rotunda*). He employed circular diagrams called 'memory wheels' with images not only for separate divisions but also for groups of divisions. He claimed that his system showed a complete picture of the universe and aimed to embrace all human knowledge within its scope.

Images typical of those employed in the round art can be seen in the circular north rose window of Chartres Cathedral. Erected in 1145, it is divided into a variety of mnemonic places with images of the Virgin and her Mother, the doves of the spirit, the kings of Israel, and the twelve prophets.

The square art was regarded as artificial and the round art as natural. The latter was also championed by Robert Fludd (1547-1637), who, however, tried to combine the two. Square buildings within circular representations of the universe were Fludd's 'Theatre of the World.'

The value of place memory has been confirmed in an experiment by Baddeley and Lieberman. They asked their subjects to memorize a series of ten items either by rote or by place memory; with the latter they imagined themselves walking through a university campus and depositing each item in one of ten previously selected spots. The results of the experiment showed that the method of place memory is of definite value in assisting subsequent recall of the items. [92]

6. Applications of Place Memory

Place memory has the advantage of random access. That is, it permits the learner to select a fact associated with a particular locus irrespective of its position in the series of loci.

Consequently, it is suitable for memorizing a number of specific items or facts, whether related to each other or not, where it is important not to have to work through the whole series from the beginning every time it is desired to recall a particular one.

It appeals particularly to the learner who is capable of visualizing the various parts of a building (or the plan of a building) and of locating in each one a specific fact which also lends itself to being easily visualized in association with that part.

If you are going to apply the method of place memory, it is best to use a location that you are thoroughly familiar with, such as your local shopping precinct, the houses round your village green, the parts of your parish church, the departments of your local supermarket or hypermarket, etc. Here is an example based on a row of premises found in a road in a small town. It is employed for solving the following problem.

'I am training to become a pharmacist,' said Mr J. A . P., 'and am in the second year of my course. I have to remember the names of a lot of medicines. I would be most obliged if you could show me a precise way of improving my memory for medicines.'

Let us take as our example the following short list of common drugs:

Ventolin
Becotide
Intal
Penbritin
Erythromycin
Choledyl

We can learn the above list with the help of the place-memory method as follows:

Place	Name of Drug	Memory image
Café	Ventolin	Ventilate your coffee to cool it.
Pet shop	Becotide	Pets swim in beckoning tide.
Shipping agents	Intal	International trade.
Stationer	Penbritin	Pen in brightly-lit window.
Solicitor's office	Erythromycin	Consult a solicitor about my sin.
Chemist	Choledyl	Co(mpany) led (the) ill.

Here are some places of common occurrence which will be found useful in applying the above method:

Town hall, public library, bookseller, museum, art gallery, police station, fire station, railway station, bus station, disco, cinema, theatre, hotel, café, restaurant, department store, supermarket, sports centre, sauna.

Health food store, shopping precinct, grammar school,

comprehensive school, junior school, infants school, college, cathedral, church, chapel, garage, filling station, swimming-bath, park, market place, post office, travel agent, baker, confectioner.

Tobacconist, newsagent, bingo hall, record shop, radio & TV shop, fish & chip shop, health centre, hospital, highways depot, car park, florist, greetings card shop, public hall, dry cleaner, laundrette, hardware shop, Co-op, photographer, public house.

Furniture store, bank, newspaper office, old folks' home, day nursery, factory, warehouse, Jobcentre, funeral director, D-I-Y shop, hairdresser, cattle market, fishmonger, butcher, grocer, fruiterer, greengrocer, gents' outfitters, ladies' wear.

Citizens' advice bureau, taxi office, dentist, vet, zoo, cycle shop, block of flats, car accessory shop, timber merchant, builder, decorator, computer shop, gas showroom, electricity showroom, Boots, Woolworth, Marks & Spencers, British Home Stores, toy shop.

7. Word Places

A modern version of place memory employs words as loci. A simple way of selecting these is to rhyme them with the cardinal numbers, e.g., one = gun; two = shoe; three = tree; four = door; five = hive; six = sticks; seven = heaven; eight = gate; nine = wine; ten = pen; eleven = Devon; twelve = delve. This yields as verbal loci eleven concrete nouns and an action verb, all of which can readily be turned into mental images. These can then be used to form associations with a list of twelve items to be learned. The method does not work successfully beyond twelve. What happens if the list to be learned contains more than twelve items will be explained below.

Here is the word-place method employed for memorizing the following data from zoology:

Trypanosoma gambiense, which is responsible for the dread tropical disease, sleeping sickness, makes regions of West and Central Africa, where it occurs, practically uninhabitable by man. Not all trypanosomes are pathogenic, however, though many occur in the blood of vertebrates, and near relatives of trypanosomes are found in some invertebrates.

One of the important characteristics of the genus trypanosoma is that it is polymorphic, that is, the form of its body and the arrangement of the organelles vary with different stages in the life history. These variants are structurally related in a readily understandable way, and can thus be regarded as modifications of a plan common to the genus throughout its life cycle, the simpler forms being easily derivable from the more complex and vice versa.

The adult form of trypanosome proper consists of a fusiform protoplasmic body, pointed at both ends, the shape maintained by the presence of a firm pellicle. Within the cytoplasm is a large single nucleus. Arising from one end — the hinder end during movement — is a long, protoplasmic, filamentous structure, the flagellum, which is continued along the whole length of the body. Throughout the greater part of its length it is joined to the cytoplasm of the body, which is, so to speak, pulled out to form the undulating membrane. At the base of the flagellum is a darkly staining granule called the blepharoplast, and, in addition to the nucleus, there may be present, usually in relation with the flagellum, a parabasal body.

The trypanosomes swim freely in the blood plasma, not only by vibratile movements of the undulating membrane and flagellum, but also by the whole body being thrown into waves. The animals feed by absorbing food dissolved in the blood of their hosts.

Word place	Data	Memory image
Gun	Sleeping sickness	Shot by gun, dead man appears asleep.
Shoe	West and Central Africa	Shaped like a shoe.
Tree	Blood of vertebrates	Tree smeared with blood.
Door	Polymorphic body	Passing through door.
Hive	Simpler from more complex	Simple entrance to hive but complex within.
Sticks	Pointed at both ends	Obvious association.
Heaven	Single nucleus	Heaven nucleus of Christian aspirations.
Gate	Long flagellum	Like a long gate.
Wine	Darkly staining granule	Dark like red wine in glass.
Pen	Parabasal body	Like the stand on which a pen rests.

Word place	*Data*	*Memory image*
Devon	Swim freely	In the rivers of Devon.
Delve	Feed on hosts' blood	They delve into it for nourishment.

The effectiveness of this method has been investigated by Bugelski, Kidd, and Segmen. They asked their subjects to learn 10-word lists. Each word was paired with an item in the word-place list. The subjects were instructed to associate the two by combining them in a mental image. Their performance was compared with that of a control group who did not use the word-place method.

The conclusion of the experiment was that this is a highly effective mnemonic device. It was found that the word lists were far better remembered with the aid of the word places than without them, provided that subjects were allowed enough time to form their mental pictures. The experimenters found that, when the words were presented at a fast rate of one every 2 seconds, there was little difference between the experimental and the control groups: both recalled only just over 40 per cent of the words correctly. But when the rate was slowed down to one word every 4 seconds, the mnemonic group remembered 80 per cent while the control group remembered only 60 per cent. And when the words were presented at the rate of one every 8 seconds, the mnemonic group recalled nearly 100 per cent while the control group still remembered only 70 per cent.[93]

We promised above to explain what happens if the list to be learned with the help of the word-place method contains more than twelve items. This apparent obstacle can be overcome in a quite simple way. Bower and Reitman have indicated how it can be done by instructing their subjects to add each further item to one of the mental images already formed. For example, suppose that 'employment' has previously been associated with 'gun', and then a thirteenth item, say, 'helicopter', is required to be learned. This can be associated with both 'gun' and 'employment' — by imagining that the employment of a gun is to shoot down a helicopter. Any further items in a list longer than twelve can be treated in the same way.

Bower and Reitman found that all the lists of words were better remembered by subjects who had elaborated their original mental pictures in this way than they were by subjects who started again with the original word-places, ignoring the first set of items that they had memorized.[94]

8. Letter Places

The method described above uses words as memory places. It is possible to adapt it equally successfully to letters. In this case the mnemonic is formed from the letters that spell a single word, phrase, or short sentence. The spelling itself forms the unity that holds the letters together.

In 1978 archaeologists excavating the Roman fort in Manchester found a fragment of pottery inscribed with part of a well-known cryptogram or word square which has been noted in inscriptions discovered elsewhere in the Roman Empire. In full it reads:

```
R O T A S
O P E R A
T E N E T
A R E P O
S A T O R
```

The word square is scratched on a piece of plaster exhibited in the Corinium Museum in Cirencester. This is ascribed by archaeologists to the 2nd or 3rd century AD. Excavations at Pompeii revealed it scratched on a column in the gymnasium there. From the number of such inscriptions which have been unearthed, it seems clear that it was of wide currency in the ancient world.

The words are Latin and can be read across, down, up, or backwards. Whichever way they are read, the translation is the same. It is: 'Arepo, the sower, holds the wheels (i.e., guides the plough) as his work.'

```
                    A
                    P
                    A
                    T
                    E
                    R
A  P A T E R N O S T E R O
                    O
                    S
                    T
                    E
                    R
                    O
```

The use to which it was put is disputed. Some authorities see it employed as a magic talisman. Christians find meaning in it as a double anagram of the first two words of the Lord's Prayer, combined with the first and last letters of the Greek alphabet, i.e., A(lpha) and O(mega), signifying the beginning and end (of all things).

That the Roman Catholic church accepts this interpretation is reflected in the fact that the square decorated the front of the altar cloth at an open-air mass celebrated by Pope John Paul II during his visit to England in 1982.

It is tempting to suppose, however, that the cryptogram may have had some more mundane practical use than this. It may, in fact, be a memory device based on the use of individual letters as places. That is, each point in the material to be recalled could be associated with one of the letters of the inscription. The points would be stated in the form of Latin words, phrases, or sentences, each of which began with one of the letters.

If this is indeed a mnemonic system, it is equally well adapted to learning material in English. For instance, suppose we wish to memorize twenty-five points about memory itself. We might utilize the twenty-five letters of the inscription as follows:

R emembering is an activity rather than a faculty of the mind.

O ut of the question to improve the brain's sheer power of retention.

T o remember better, improve methods of learning.

A cts both backwards and forwards, using lessons of past to plan for future.

S o defined as attending to a mental image determined by a past experience.

O rganized in three modes: input, processing, output.

P rofessor, absent-minded for some things, retentive of others, shows memory not unitary.

E xperiences of forgetting caused by weak impression, disuse, interference, repression.

R ecall is affected soon after learning.

A fter learning, immediate revision advisable to delay forgetting.

T V advertising relies heavily upon importance of repetition in remembering.

E xample of Berlioz: repressed idea for a symphony because it impeded support of sick wife.

N ever happier was Thomas Hood than in his childhood remembered in his poetry.

E arly childhood forgotten because brain, ideas of self, and verbal ability not developed.

T hreatened by birth of sibling, Goethe recalled early memory of throwing crockery.

A s aid to concentration, important to make it a habit.

R elaxation also important in concentration.

E motional conflict should be avoided because it diverts attention from work in hand.

P resence of interest in the material also essential for concentration.

O ften possible to devise simple mnemonics, e.g., 'separate' or 'seperate'? (mnemonic: part).

S teps for remembering are:

A ttention to the material is essential.

T o develop a keen interest is vital.

O pen the mind to forming associations that will ensure recall.

R epetition with intention to remember is also important.

The above example illustrates one of three forms which the method can take, i.e., where the cue letters do not spell the name of the topic to be memorized. Indeed, in this example they are not even in the same language. The second type occurs where the cue letters neither name the subject-matter nor are meaningful in themselves. An example of this is the mnemonic SPLINK used for memorizing the Green Cross code and described earlier in this chapter. The third type is used when the letter-place phrase or sentence is both meaningful and directly related to the subject-matter of the material.

9. Using Letter Places in Learning

This last-mentioned refinement can be recommended to students faced with the task of memorizing written lecture notes or printed textbook matter, especially in the large quantities associated with examination syllabuses.

What do you know about osmosis? Flat foot? Methotamine? The Highway Code? The dogmatic policy? The career of Ovid? Holding companies? Rheumatoid arthritis? Digestion in the stomach? The murder of Julius Caesar? The liquid drop model of the nucleus? The flora and fauna of cold regions? Flash, fire and ignition temperature? The effects of working on the structure of a metal? Internal control in a computer-based accounting system? The duties and powers of local authorities in regard to rubbish on vacant land?

You may be quite an authority on one or more of these subjects; on the other hand, you may claim that you know nothing at all about any of them. But is this strictly true? Even if you have never studied any of these topics, can you truthfully say that you know nothing about them? The answer is that you cannot. Let me explain.

Even if you have never looked at a book in any of the above fields, you can still be said to know something about all of them. What you know at the very least is the names of the subjects. For instance, what you know about holding companies is the phrase 'holding companies'. That at least is a start. Moreover, you haven't even had to remember it: I have (or the examiner has) given it to you in the wording of the question. In fact, every examiner must inevitably give away something in setting examination questions at all. He must disclose the topics that the questions deal with.

Let us assume that all you know about, say, methotamine is just the name of the drug. Now, suppose that from the name of this (or any other topic) you could reconstruct the information that you need to be able to answer an examination question on the topic. For instance, if, starting just from the word 'methotamine,' you could recall the details of dosage, actions, uses, and toxic and side effects, you could be said to remember all that you need to know about the drug.

Or let us assume that all you know about digestion in the stomach is the two words 'stomach' and 'digestion'. If from these two words you could reconstruct the facts about this physiological process, you could be said to remember those facts. I think you would agree that, if this were possible, it would be an extremely useful accomplishment.

Again, suppose that, given the phrase 'rubbish on vacant land' — or just one word of it — you could from this simple fact recall everything you knew about the topic, answering a question on it would prove to be no trouble at all to you in your examination.

What I am suggesting is that you need to organize your knowledge in such a way that the examination question itself forms a starting-point, setting off a train of thought which will enable you to recall the information needed to answer it properly.

Fortunately, there is a way in which this can be done. The letter-place method of the third type mentioned above permits you to do just what we have described. It involves learning your material by associating one point in it with each of the letters of a matrix word, phrase, or sentence which summarizes the contents of the subject-matter. All you do is to start with a word or phrase that embodies the name of the topic you want to remember. You use each individual letter of that word or phrase as a key to recall a point that you have previously associated with it.

In this method there are no non-significant letters. All letters of the alphabet are equally significant, and the fact that they may not be pronounced in a word does not matter. Whether they are pronounced or not, they can all serve as cues. The cue letters are provided by whatever word, phrase, or sentence covers all the facts in your notes. *Each letter is linked to one point in the material by stating the point in the form of a sentence which begins with that letter.* This sounds a little complicated when described, but the actual application of the method is simpler than the description suggests.

The word 'matrix' means literally a mould into which something is cast or shaped. The method provides a way of casting your knowledge into a mould that helps you to recall it. If your knowledge is linked in this way with topics that will be given to you by the examiner, you can recall your material by reminding yourself of the points which you have associated with the letters comprising your key word, phrase, or sentence.

For instance, consider the following question:

> What precautions should be taken to prevent sparks from ferrous material or foreign substances causing possible fire hazards?

This is a question of the type that one can reasonably expect to come across in the examination taken by firemen. There are, in fact, four volumes studied by firemen, each of which contains 1001 questions of this type.

What information is the examiner giving away in asking this question? He is giving away the fact that the question deals with fire risks from ferrous materials. Now, if you are a fireman, you will, during your examination preparation, have studied the facts which you are required to produce in order to answer this question. You can more readily reproduce them if you have previously organized those facts in accordance with the letter-place method.

Let us see how this method works out in detail by taking as our example Unit 1 of an Open University Foundation Course in the Social Sciences. This deals with 'The Fundamentals of Human Nature.' The first thing to do is to read the material and summarize it. Its main contents can be summarized in twenty points as follows:

WHY DO MEN LIVE IN SOCIETIES?

1. Psychology understands the mind by studying and explaining the behaviour of living organisms.
2. Observation and experiment can discover laws which govern the behaviour of man as well as lower animals.
3. Instinctive behaviour tends to emerge in a mature form at birth, for example, the bee dance.
4. Instinctive behaviour is identical in all members of a given species.
5. In instinctive behaviour the sequence of actions performed depends upon the right stimulus being present at exactly the right time.
6. Lower animals have a limited choice of behaviour whereas man is capable of modifying his behaviour by learning.
7. Learning is the organization of a system which tends to carry out one sort of behaviour under one set of circumstances.
8. This enables man to achieve 'socialization', much of human social behaviour being learned rather than genetically determined.
9. Bodily needs produce drives impelling the organism to activity which reduces the need.
10. Inborn basic drives upon which individual survival depends are to breathe, drink, eat, excrete, rest, and avoid pain.
11. Partially inborn drives upon which survival of species depends are to mate and care for young.
12. Inborn and learned drives upon which survival of the individual and species depends are to escape, attack, explore, and seek sensory stimulation.

13. Learned drives upon which depends survival of society are to praise, achieve, dominate, submit, acquire, belong, help.
14. Man lives in society in order to satisfy his basic needs easily.
15. The view that social drives were acquired by 'generalization' from a basic drive has been countered by experiments of Harlows (1962) and Fantz (1966).
16. Experimental demonstrations of learned drives, e.g. fear, are plentiful.
17. Society creates these drives and uses them to train the individual to accept its values.
18. Man thus lives in society because he receives his social rewards from it.
19. Language facilitates changes of behaviour through the influence of one person on another.
20. Written language permits the communication of discoveries from one generation to another.

Now, how are we to remember these twenty points? With the help of the letter-place method we can not only recall the points in sequence but also achieve random access to any particular point. As there are twenty of them, we choose as our cue-letter matrix a phrase or sentence containing 20 letters. WHY MAN LIVES IN SOCIETY will do admirably for this purpose. We remember each point by associating it with its appropriate letter in this phrase as follows:-

W hat psychology does is understand the mind by studying and explaining behaviour.

H ow laws govern behaviour can be discovered by observation and experiment.

Y et even at birth instinctive behaviour emerges in mature form.

M embers of given species all show identical instinctive behaviour.

A ction sequence in instinctive behaviour depends upon right stimulus at right time.

N o great choice of behaviour for lower animals, but man can modify behaviour by learning.

L earning is organization of system carrying out one sort of behaviour under one set of circumstances.

I t enables man to achieve 'socialization.'

V arious bodily needs produce drives.

E ndogenous basic drives for individual survival are to breathe, drink, eat, excrete, rest, and avoid pain.

S pecies-survival partially inborn drives are to mate and care for young.

I nborn and learned drives for individul and species survival are to escape, attack, explore, and seek sensory stimulation.

N umerous learned drives for survival of society are to praise, achieve, dominate, submit, acquire, belong, help.

S atisfying basic needs easily is why man lives in society.

O bjection to view that social drives acquired by 'generalization' (Harlows, Fantz).

C onfirmation of learned drives by experimental evidence.

I n creating these drives, society also uses them to train the individual.

E njoying social rewards, man lives in society.

T hrough influence of one person on another, language facilitates changes of behaviour.

Y ear by year through generations written language communicates discoveries.

You can easily see the advantage of putting your material in this form. Having attached one point to each letter, you have a matrix which summarizes the entire material and serves as a framework for remembering it.

Now what do you do when faced with a question in the examination room? All you have to do is to hold in mind the letter-place word, phrase, or sentence. This will probably be given to you by the examiner in his wording of the question. Even if it isn't, you can easily remember it because it is closely related to your subject-matter. Then mentally work through the letters, reviving the points which you have previously associated with them. Each letter will remind you of a word that begins with that letter, and each word is the first word of a statement embodying the point to be recalled. This recall provides you with the facts which you need to answer an examination question on the subject.

The method is equally suitable for a written examination or for a viva voce. What is more, it enables you to remember the material in sequential order, or it gives you random access to any point in the matrix. That is, you can either remember it in sequence, starting from the first letter of your phrase, or you can pick upon any individual letter, thus recalling any point out of order. It is not necessary to start from the beginning of the phrase each time.

Large amounts of material, such as are found in an examination syllabus, call for a learning technique that is concise and economical. The above method meets this requirement.

Enough has now been said to justify the usefulness and conciseness of the letter-place method. It should be obvious to you that the method can equally well be applied to your own examination studies. You will find it invaluable regardless of what you are studying — Sartre's ontological dimensions, Kant's transcendental deductions, the stationary points of a function of several variables, consignments inwards, food preparation, book-keeping to the balance sheet, or whatever. I suggest that you now try it for yourself. Just select as your matrix the word or phrase which best fits the material. Then use the letters in the word or phrase to enable you to remember the points in the material in the manner described above.

As you can see, the method makes use of verbal associations; it involves no visualizing of mental pictures. This is an obvious advantage when we are dealing with many examination subjects, e.g., philosophy, which are too abstract to lend themselves to mental-picture making.

A student to whom letter-places were recommended said: 'I would like to thank you for showing me how to deal with my study materials. I found your method very interesting and helpful.'

Another student reported: 'Thank you very much for a different way of handling study material. I have already tried it on different passages. It works just fine. I find it easier to remember the material that I have learnt. It saves me a lot of trouble.'

A lady who used the letter-place method reported: 'I appreciate your help very much and already feel that, whereas before there seemed so much to carry in mind, it now seems much more organized. My massive reading is now much more interesting.'

Another student stated: 'Your information, I am sure, will be of great help to me in my examinations this November. It would seem that the principle of learning and remembering the contents of textbooks is to employ a key which is both very logical and very practical.'

5.

The Technique of Passing Exams

You are reading this book because you are keen to apply its methods of learning academic ideas, facts, and figures with a minimum expenditure of time and effort. This chapter in particular will appeal to you if, as is probable, you are in a position similar to the ones described by students in the following reports.

'I have recently started studying for an examination,' said a 19-year-old insurance clerk, Mr P. R. S., 'but I find that the work I do one week is forgotten the following week, although at the time I know it sufficiently well to be able to answer questions on it.'

'I shall shortly be sitting,' said a student, 'for my General Certificate of Education at Ordinary level. I need to remember factual information, such as experiments, laws, and formulae in chemistry. Can you please advise me on how I can do this?'

Another student reported: 'In two weeks' time I shall be commencing a full-time course of study for a professional qualifying examination. I have six law subjects to learn and the course consists of one or two one-hour lectures each day. The remainder of the day is spent in preparing for the next day's lecture and in learning what has been taught that day. Retaining what one has been taught from the notes taken at the lectures is vital. I enclose a few pages of the type of material which I shall need to learn. These are only sub-headings and notes will be dictated under each.'

He enclosed typewritten pages relating to two of the six subjects which comprised his course. They consisted of subject headings on conveyancing taken from a textbook on this subject by Gibson and on revenue law taken from another textbook by Pinson. Readers who are students of law will doubtless be familiar with these authorities.

A fourth student said: 'Learning and memory skills, the visual presentation of learning materials, and "internal representations" (the way in which we internalize or "model" our experience) are all of particular interest to me. My work as a research student involves the development of more effective teaching systems. Thus my concern is with attention, learning, and memory mechanisms as applied to study materials.'

'You will agree,' he continued, 'that few students are required to store material for verbatim recall. The student is required to abstract higher-order characteristics of a generalizable kind. In short, he is expected to "understand" rather than to "memorize". I'm sure that you acknowledge the possibility of improvement or development in the direction I have indicated.'

These requests embody typical problems facing thousands of candidates — problems that are apt to grow more acute as their examination draws nearer. They are looking for something more than the techniques which they have been taught at school. What you need as a student is something that will enable you to understand and retain information and ideas in a quick, practical way. In these chapters we are endeavouring to answer this need.

Examinations are an accepted feature of the modern scene whether we like them or not. Their influence upon our future can often be decisive. Promotion prospects may largely depend upon them in many careers. Knowing how to approach and sit for them is an essential part of the technique of study. This is what will be discussed in the present chapter.

Passing an examination calls for a familiarity with the material learned during the course and the ability to compare, criticize, discuss, explain, etc. the topics proposed in the examination questions.

A basic essential is a keen interest in the subject or subjects you are studying. If you lack this, you can cultivate it by thinking about your reason for studying. Preferably you should have several good reasons. You should be able to see the value of the material by relating it to your own life. You should have a definite purpose in view and should hold in your mind a clear picture of yourself achieving that purpose. Think of what it will mean to you when you succeed. As advised in Chapter 3, repeat to yourself: 'This subject is useful to me and I like it more each day.'

1. How to Make Notes

It is more than a coincidence that there are addicts of the notebook habit among the great minds of the world. A list of inveterate note-takers would include such famous names as Charles Darwin, Robert Louis Stevenson, Émile Zola, Thomas Hobbes, Jonathan Edwards, Isaac Newton, Albert Einstein. Notes serve four main purposes:

(a) They constitute a written record which can be first learned and later revised.

(b) They express your understanding of the material in your own words.

(c) They help you to remember the main ideas and important details.

(d) They provide the raw material for a more formal treatment of the subject, such as in an essay.

So make notes on the content of what you have read or heard. There are two ways of doing this.

One is to write a précis or summary in continuous prose. If you adopt this method, write short, simple sentences. Use short, common words as far as the subject-matter permits. Both sentence complexity and word rarity are known to make notes hard to understand and remember. Write in the active rather than the passive voice. That is, write 'The topic sentence states the main idea' rather than 'The main idea is stated in the topic sentence.' A study by Smith and McMahon has shown that when people read a sentence and then answer a question on it, it takes them 15 per cent longer to answer if the sentence is in the passive voice.

The other method is to break up the ideas into main points and major details. You can then produce a skeleton outline employing lettered and/or numbered headings and sub-headings indented at varying distances from the left margin. Make sure that you include everything important. This method has the advantage that it makes for greater clarity. It enables you to appreciate the logical arrangement and classification of the material.

You can take your notes on separate sheets which can be kept in a loose-leaf binder. Or you can make them in a bound notebook. The latter is probably neater and more manageable, but the former has the advantage of greater flexibility. It permits you to arrange and rearrange your notes to suit the growing state of your knowledge.

In your notes make use of abbreviations that you can understand. Standard abbreviations like 'i.e.' and 'e.g.' can be employed. A common practice in abbreviating both long and short words is to leave out the vowels, e.g. wds. (words), lgcl. (logical), etc.

The use of capital letters, underlining, putting words in boxes, drawings, and diagrams all contribute to making notes easier to picture in the mind. And there is no doubt that being able to see a page of notes in the mind is an invaluable aid in remembering them.

For example, a student said: 'I am in my last year of a Ph.D. in horticulture at Nottingham University. I have found that my most reliable means of remembering my notes is to use coloured ink and then virtually photograph the page in my mind. I suppose I was associating what I remembered with its position on a page.'

2. Learning your Notes

Previous chapters of this book have put forward a number of suggestions intended to be helpful for this purpose. Some of the more important of these hints (with additional comments relevant to exam needs) are:

1. Always make an effort to understand the material, especially the principles which underlie it.
2. Study a little at a time at fairly frequent intervals. This is better than studying for long stretches at a time with longish intervals between your study periods. A few minutes every day devoted to your studies will produce better results than a week of neglect followed by several hours of intensive work. It is the thing which you do consistently every day for fifteen minutes which is more beneficial to you than that which you forget for a week and then work on diligently for three hours.
3. Instead of reading and rereading, read and then try to recall. The popular way of doing a thing is not always the best way. For instance, people may expect to remember a piece of material after reading it once — or after reading it and then rereading it. Both methods are inadequate, the first because it is not thorough enough and the second because it is an uneconomical use of time. Research has shown that a second reading brings only 7 per cent more comprehension, while a third one adds

only another 1 per cent. The time spent on rereading is out of proportion to the gain that can be expected from it. A better method is known as the P-V formula.

(a) *P stands for Preview.* Browse through the material to get a general idea of what it is about. Close the book and think about what you have gathered from your preview.

(b) *Q stands for Question.* Ask yourself a few questions which you want your reading to answer. Some authors suggest such questions at the beginning of a chapter. If your author doesn't, think of your own.

(c) *R stands for Read.* Read the material and make sure that you understand it. Underline key words and/or phrases. Think about what you have read. Assess the relative importance of its various features.

(d) *S stands for Summarize.* Make notes on what you read, summarizing the material in either or both of the two ways we have suggested.

(e) *T stands for Test.* Test yourself on what you have read by using the information to answer the questions you asked under Q (above). Answer questions and problems set by your lecturer or by your textbook author. Answer questions set in earlier exam papers. Refer to what critics have said about the material and ask youself whether you agree with them. Discuss the subject with someone.

(f) *U stands for Use.* Try to put the material to some practical use in everyday affairs.

(g) *V stands for Visualize.* Picture the ideas in your mind's eye. Or visualize the actual pages of the textbook or notebook.

Preview, Question, Read, Summarize, Test, Use, Visualize — these are your keys to more efficient study. Established by experimental research on learning methods, the P-V formula has proved its value in understanding and retaining what you read.

4.   Material is forgotten more slowly when it is 'overlearned' (more than barely learned). This means that you should not study your material until you only just know it, but until you know it very well. This will tend to ensure that you remember it better.

5. Which are you more interested in: the study itself or what it can do for you? If the former, you may learn the material better if you break off your study before you come to a natural division of the subject-matter, e.g., the end of a section. On the other hand, if you are more interested in what the course can do for you, you may learn it better if you carry on to the end of the section or chapter.

6. If you study in the evening, go to bed afterwards rather than take up further waking activity, especially of a similar kind. Revise the material in the morning before the activity of the day makes you forget too much of it. Revision is most economical when carried out as soon as possible after learning. The reason for this is that the material is forgotten rapidly in the first few hours after learning, and then more and more slowly. In other words, most of what you lose is lost the same week.

    If one period of study must be immediately followed by another, try to ensure, if possible, that it is of a different sort or in a different subject. Avoid other mental work, especially of a similar kind, in the event that you cannot go to bed immediately after studying.

7. If possible, study at the same table or desk or while sitting in the same chair. This, too, tends to help recall of the material.

8. Lightly brace yourself (but not too much) as you work.

9. The autosuggestion 'I can study and assimilate' has a definitely positive effect in improving both concentration and retention. 'Autosuggestion has helped my memory in everyday affairs,' reported Mr E. C.

10. It is also advisable to put in plenty of practice at answering questions set in previous examination papers in order to get your mind adjusted to the 'feel' of the examination conditions.

3. How to Revise

Two psychologists, Davis and Moore, cited by Laird and Laird, compared the rate of forgetting of meaningless material with that of meaningful material. They found that with meaningful material the initial loss was less after one day and after one month than with meaningless material. They also noted that between six months and one year after learning there was even a slight improvement in the recall of meaningful material as compared with meaningless material. [95]

Consequently, it is most economical to refresh our memory of study material as soon as possible after we have studied it, rather than to wait until some time has elapsed. The practical corollary for the examination candidate is that revision should be done not only at the end of your course but at intervals while the course is in progress. In this way you will at all stages establish a firm foundation of knowledge to which you can constantly add new facts as you learn them.

An investigation of differences in study habits showed that among successful students the habit of revising notes the same day was nearly three times commoner than among failing students.

Accepting the fact that memory starts to fall as soon as learning is completed and that the fall is rapid at first but levels out later, Tony Buzan in his *Use Your Head* recommends what he calls 'a programmed pattern of review'. [96]

'The first review,' he writes, 'should take place about 10 minutes after a one-hour learning period and should itself take 10 minutes. This will keep the recall high for approximately one day, when the next review should take place, this time for a period of 2 to 4 minutes. After this, recall will probably be retained for approximately a week, when another 2-minute review can be completed followed by a further review after about one month. After this the knowledge will be lodged in Long Term Memory.'

In his book Buzan makes much of what is known as the reminiscence effect. This was first discovered by Ballard in 1913. He found that his subjects, who were young children, appeared to remember more poetry a day or two after the last learning period than they did when they were tested immediately after the learning period. [97]

This conclusion, however, is not properly supported by the experimental findings of psychologists. McGeoch found that 84 per cent of a group of young subjects admitted that they had mentally rehearsed the memorized material during the interval between learning and testing. [98] Melton and Stone carried out an experiment designed to exclude this factor. They had their subjects employed in naming colours during the interval. When this was done, no reminiscence effect was found. [99]

This suggests that the improved recall between the learning period and the test was due not to the reminiscence effect, as Buzan supposes, but to mental rehearsal or revision of the material. Buzan gives the right advice but bases it on the wrong reason.

Buzan's error is repeated by R. Freeman in *Mastering Study Skills*. Freeman prints a graph which purports to show that after one day recall has dropped to about 80 per cent but that revision at that point immediately brings it back to 100 per cent. One week after this first revision, recall has again dropped to only 80 per cent and is immediately restored to 100 per cent by a second revision period. One month later, when it has fallen to only about 95 per cent, a third revision again restores it to 100 per cent. The graph suggests that about midway between the second and third revision sessions the amount of recall actually increases slightly. Here again the message is that reliance should be placed upon the proven value of continuous revision rather than upon the unproven reminiscence effect. [100]

Bugelski, however, has pointed out that, if we test the same subject on the same material at different intervals, the tests themselves act as a form of revision. In these circumstances, the rate of forgetting is slowed down although there is still an initial sharp drop immediately after learning. [101]

As Ian M. L. Hunter puts it in his *Memory Facts and Fallacies*, 'The facilitating effect of successive testing on retention is analogous to the value of periodic review in formal study or teaching. A student, for example, who hears a lecture and must answer questions on it a week later, does better if he thinks over the lecture each day trying to recall the points made and the topics discussed than if he merely attempts to recall it in the exam without previous review.' [102]

It is as well to revise material from each of several lessons rather than from one lesson only. Discussing it with someone else who is interested in it can be a useful means of revision. Don't rely only on silent reading or rereading. Repeat your material aloud or run over it silently from memory. Try to look at it from more than one angle or to combine various points in different ways.

A big drawback that the examination candidate faces is that his revision material is no longer fresh. You find yourself reluctant to revise your notes because revision is rather boring compared with the original learning. It is, therefore, often helpful to try to reorganize the old material to imbue it with some of the freshness that it now lacks. The methods described in this book are recommended partly with the aim of making notes more interesting to refer to again.

Don't overlook the importance of that revision which takes the form of applying the material you have learned to practical situations in everyday life. Look for opportunities of using it in this way. By doing so, you make it truly your own and guarantee that your mastery of it stays with you for a long time to come.

4. In the Examination Hall

(a) *Mental attitude*
Have confidence in your ability to do your best. If you feel nervous at the thought of the approaching examination, the thing to do is to have made yourself thoroughly familiar with the syllabus beforehand. This puts you in a position to say to yourself: 'If I don't pass, no one will!' Remember that the examiner is not there to fail you. He wants to see if you have prepared yourself adequately and to give you an opportunity of showing this. He wants to know if you can answer certain selected topics logically, thoughtfully, and pointedly. The questions are the outcome of a great deal of preliminary discussion among the examiners. They aim to be fair, to cover various aspects of the syllabus, and to reward competent answers.

(b) *Reading the paper*
When the paper is handed to you, read it carefully. Don't lose marks unnecessarily by failing to observe the examiner's instructions. If he asks you to *explain*, don't *describe*. If short notes are called for, don't write long ones. If you are required to give examples, make sure that they are relevant. A well-chosen example at any point will always secure more marks than a bald statement.

Read every question carefully before you attempt to answer it. One question may spark off ideas which will be useful to you in answering another. Make a sensible choice of optional questions. Avoid a question that appears to you to be at all ambiguous. Before tackling any question, decide exactly what the examiner wants. Say to yourself: 'What is he asking for?' Having settled this, give it to him in your answer.

(c) *Presenting your answer*
Adopt a methodical approach in answering a question. Avoid a slipshod

presentation of your work. Write legibly. Number or letter your points. Use headings. Clear arrangement in your written answers is a distinct advantage. Make it easy for the examiner to see what you are getting at. Make sure that your answer is relevant to the question actually asked.

If a question is in more than one part, consider each part well in relation to the others. This will help to save you from giving irrelevant answers. A Joint Matriculation Board report on GCE scripts complains: 'As usual, there was a common failure to focus upon the questions as such . . . Too many candidates were determined to regurgitate information rather than to answer the question.'

(d) *Time*
Don't spend too much time on any one question. Leave a little time at the end for rereading both the paper and your answers. You may be able to obtain extra marks by correcting obvious mistakes and omissions. If necessary, you can write in the margin — but write clearly. Correct any mis-spellings or faulty grammar. Put your punctuation right. Get the examiner on your side by making your answers as easy to read as you can.

5. How to Answer Essay-type Exams
There are several further points worth remembering when an examination paper of this common type is placed before you.

(e) *Outline*
Have an outline of the course in your mind when you enter the examination room. This you will have prepared during your studies leading up to the exam. You will have done it by taking notes during lectures, underlining key passages and making marginal notes in your textbooks, summarizing your reading, and revising your material periodically. Someone has said that the successful candidate usually passes an exam several months before he sits for it. Thorough preparation in the period preceding the examination is the best way of guaranteeing success.

(f) *Terms of reference*
Certain terms crop up regularly in exam papers, e.g. analyse, comment, criticize, discuss, illustrate, justify, outline, prove. Get clear in your

mind the differences of meaning among them. We will examine some of these terms in a later section of this chapter.

(g) *Selection*
Before beginning to write, select the headings and material for your answer. Organize them intelligently and systematically — either in your head or on a piece of scrap paper. Arrange them in logical order, starting a fresh paragraph with each new topic. Supply details and examples to support general statements. For example, a question might be handled by defining some term to begin with, going on to develop your ideas about it, and concluding by saying whether the use of the term is justified or not.

(h) *Conciseness*
Write concisely. Wordiness and padding are weaknesses in an exam essay, as indeed they are in any piece of writing. Remember that examiners are adept at spotting waffle. Try to show as clearly and concisely as possible that you have read up the particular topic and have some understanding of it.

(i) *Flexibility*
As you write, other ideas may occur to you. So keep your outline flexible enough to permit you to incorporate them.

(j) *Summary notes*
If you run short of time and can't put all your ideas down in essay form, include them in summary form. Here the notes you have prepared for revision purposes will come in useful. This will at least show the examiner that you are familiar with the material. Then press on with the next question.

Freeman points out the conclusions that can be drawn from the following instructions commonly found in examination papers:

1. Answer either . . . or . . .
2. Answer only five questions.
3. Answer all the questions.
4. Write short notes on . . .

He says that the first instruction implies that both parts of the question carry equal marks. You will not be penalized by answering one rather than the other — but if you answer both your second answer will be ignored.

Instruction 2 implies that all the questions in the paper carry the same marks. Again, if you answer more than the stipulated number, you will receive marks for only the first five.

From the third instruction it can be concluded that all the questions do *not* carry equal marks. You do not know which ones carry higher marks than the others. To fail to observe this instruction may mean omitting a question which bears the highest marks.

A question prefaced by the fourth instruction will probably contain several topics, all of which should be dealt with. Essay-type sentences are not required here. Freeman thinks that such a question probably won't earn you many marks anyway, so there is not much point in spending a great deal of time on it. [103]

6. More About Terms

Examiners are fond of beginning questions with certain stock verbs like 'Explain . . .', 'Discuss . . .', 'State . . .', and so on. It is, therefore, worth while studying the differences between these verbs, so as to make sure that in your answer you are doing what you are supposed to do. There is no point in describing if you are asked to prove, nor in enumerating if you are required to criticize. Unless you adhere precisely to the terms of the question, you are likely to lose marks.

Comment is an ambiguous verb because it means both 'write explanatory notes' and 'criticize'. So the examiner may expect you to do both and penalize you if you don't. For this reason questions which ask you to comment are perhaps best avoided if you have a choice.

Compare means 'State how two things resemble or are related to each other,' e.g.,

> Like all creatures, man must come to terms with his environment. Unlike other animal species, he has learned to control that environment to a great degree.

Criticize means 'Express an opinion about.' This word should not be restricted to its everyday meaning, which is 'Express an adverse opinion about'. Here is an example of criticism:

> The association of Cleopatra's Needle with Cleopatra is uncertain. The name is misleading as this obelisk dates from a very much earlier period than the reign of that ill-fated queen.

Define means 'Give the exact meaning of '. For example:

> What does Matthew mean when he quotes Isaiah as saying: 'The virgin will conceive'? He was quoting from a Greek translation of the Old Testament, but had he gone back to the original Hebrew, he would have found that Isaiah used 'almah', a word which means simply 'young woman'. Hebrew has a different word for 'virgin'. On this evidence it is clear that Isaiah is defining a normal birth rather than a virgin birth.

Describe means 'Tell about the features of', as in the example below.

> The National Book League is a non-profit-making society devoted to stimulating the full use and enjoyment of books. It publishes a periodical, *Books*, in addition to *Book Lists* and *Reader's Guides*. It also runs a Book Information Bureau which can provide individual reading lists on special subjects.

Discuss means 'Examine in the light of arguments for and against'. For example:

> Lawrence's most famous — and most controversial — novel is the outspoken *Lady Chatterley's Lover*. This has been condemned for its attempt to make 'four-letter' words respectable, but, contrary to popular belief, its main centre of interest is not sex, but the improvement of the condition of the working class. However, the superficial (albeit true) view that *Lady Chatterley's Lover* deals frankly with sexual relations has inspired a host of more recent imitators.

Enumerate means 'Set out in order one after the other'. *List* has the same meaning. Here is an example, which lists or enumerates the steps in a recipe:

> Select smooth, medium-sized potatoes. Wash, dry, and place in pan. Bake forty minutes or until soft in a very hot oven. Serve at once.

Evaluate, strictly speaking, means 'Count, ascertain the amount of '. In maths it means 'Find a numerical expression for'. It is also used in the sense of 'Give an opinion of '. For example:

The Robbins Report on Higher Education mentioned the need to study the economic and social problems which science students meet in their careers. This must be welcomed as implying a recognition of the importance of seeing one's specific job in relation to the whole.

Explain means 'Make known in detail' or 'Give reasons which account for', such as:

When other ancient Greek city-states were evolving from monarchies to democracies, Sparta was becoming a militaristic commune. Spartan training was pragmatic in nature although very harsh, and began at the age of seven in the case of boys. The children were subjected to the most odious experiences, including whipping and a great discomfort in all acts of mere living. The result of the training was a well-organized army of inscrutable and worthy adversaries.

Illustrate means 'Make clear by means of examples' or 'Explain by means of drawings'. Here is an example of the former meaning:

To determine the meaning of a word that has a prefix, you combine the meanings of the separate parts. For example, add 'semi-', which means 'half', to 'deponent', which means 'passive in form but active in sense'. This yields 'semi-deponent', which means 'having active forms in present tenses and passive forms with active sense in perfect tenses'.

Interpret means 'State the meaning of ', e.g.:

The sower of the good seed is the Son of Man. The field is the world: the good seed stands for the children of the Kingdom, the darnel for the children of the evil one. The enemy who sowed the darnel is the devil. The harvest is the end of time. The reapers are angels. (Matthew 13, 37-39.)

Justify means 'Give reasons in support of ' or 'Show how something is right'. For example:

When a person uses a cross or other mark instead of a signature, we commonly assume that he is illiterate. Until the end of the nineteenth century this assumption was almost always correct. Before the passing of Gladstone's Education Act in 1870, primary education was provided only by voluntary religious societies. There were great gaps in the network of voluntary schools, so that very many people were illiterate. Even as late as 1841 one out of three men and two out of five women in England and Wales signed the register with a mark when they got married.

Name means 'Give names or labels to' or 'Mention' or 'Specify':

> The literature of a language often contributes new words. Such a word is 'malapropism,' derived from the character of Mrs Malaprop in Sheridan's play *The Rivals*.

Outline and *summarize* mean the same thing, i.e. 'Give a brief account of'. *Précis*, too, has the same meaning. Here is an example which outlines, summarizes, or makes a précis of Edgar Allan Poe's *The Raven*:

> A weary student is visited, one stormy midnight, by a raven who can speak the single word 'Nevermore'. Tortured by grief over the loss of his beloved, the student questions the bird about the possibility of meeting her in another world. He is driven to wild demands by the repetition of the word, until the raven becomes a symbol of his dark doubts and frustrated longings.

Prove means 'Show why something is true.' In maths it means 'Test the accuracy of a calculation'. Study the following paragraph:

> *The Great Train Robbery*, produced in 1903 by Edwin S. Porter, was a notable achievement for several reasons. It established a tradition of Western films which has remained popular to the present day. Shot on location out of doors, it marked a departure from the painted scenery which had been used hitherto. It was also revolutionary in the sense that it succeeded in telling a connected story.

What is being proved here?

Report means 'Give a factual account of' or 'Tell something as spoken by another person' or 'Make a formal statement about', e.g.:

> The Battle of Agincourt was fought on the plain of Northern France in 1415. It was one of the major battles of the Hundred Years War between England and France. The French army was vastly superior in numbers to that of the English, who were led by their monarch, Henry V, in person. After landing at Harfleur and making a detour, the English were advancing on Calais when they were intercepted.

Review means 'Write a survey of the whole field of . . .' It therefore calls for a fairly lengthy answer.

State means 'Express fully or clearly'. For example:

> Pull the rotor arm off the distributor spindle and add a few drops of oil

around the head of the screw exposed to view. Do not remove this screw. Smear a small quantity of grease on to the distributor cam and the pivot post for the moving contact. Also add a small quantity of oil through the hole in the centre of the base plate through which the spindle passes. This is to lubricate the advance/retard mechanism.

A candidate who carefully studies these explanations and examples should be able to avoid the mistake of giving the wrong type of answer to a question.

Don't try to force a question to fit a stock answer which you have prepared. For instance, 'Satan as the hero' is a stock topic arising from Books I and II of Milton's *Paradise Lost*. But one year the examiners asked: 'How does Milton present us with a picture of Satan as an angel in defeat?' This did not prevent a lot of candidates from trotting out the stock answer on Satan as the hero.

Remember, too, that answers should be expressed in grammatical English with soundly constructed sentences and correct paragraphing and punctuation. A GCE examiner writes: 'Punctuation seems to be a lost art. Each year sees an increasing number of candidates using commas instead of full stops.' He urges candidates to avoid slang and colloquialisms. To misspell a word which actually appears in the paper itself is inexcusable. He continues: 'It was by no means uncommon to find faulty sentence construction, and even A-level candidates frequently confused "their" and "there". The classical élite, those taking Special Latin, often spelt Briton, Britain, and British with a double "t".' Truly, an examiner's lot, like a policeman's, is not a happy one.

I was once surprised to read a book of advice for examination candidates in which the author recommended a deliberate attempt to blind the examiner with science — by quoting from non-existent authorities. One feels that authors who recommend intellectual dishonesty are more interested in getting candidates through their examinations than in producing tomorrow's scientists, doctors, and engineers.

Both are important, certainly. But one should not take precedence to the detriment of the other. If you have prepared your work thoroughly, you will probably pass your examination anyway whether you heed my advice or anyone else's. That is, unless the questions or practical tests set are grossly unfair or irrelevant to the published syllabus, but this kind of upsetting experience is probably quite rare. If you haven't prepared your work thoroughly, trying to bluff your way through is an unacceptable solution likely to be quickly spotted by a discerning examiner.

On the other hand, there is no objection to taking advantage of anything which is more soundly based. For example, psychological experiments have shown that the beginning and end of a piece of text are better remembered than the middle. This implies that a candidate is likely to impress the examiner most by paying particular attention to the opening and closing paragraphs of his answer.

It is worth noting that occasionally one part of an examination paper can be used to supply the answer to another. For example, if you are uncertain about the gender of a French noun, look through the paper to see if it is used by the examiner in a context which makes the gender clear.

Again, in an examination for the Certificate of Proficiency in English, a question asked candidates to complete the sentence 'The course . . . of a series of lectures followed by practical demonstrations.' The expected answer, out of a choice of five optional answers, was 'consisted'. Candidates could hardly fail to get this question right if they noticed that the construction 'consisted of' occurred twice elsewhere in the same paper. One wonders whether the examiners were unaware of this or whether they had included it deliberately in order to penalize those candidates who got the question wrong for lack of observation as well as inaccuracy.

7. Concluding Advice

Can examination questions be spotted by studying previous papers and noting what has not been asked in recent years? This practice has its advocates among schoolmasters, but in my opinion it is a waste of time. A question is just as likely to be avoided as to be repeated. Moreover, the practice assumes that the same examiners will be setting this year's paper as set last year's or the year's before that. I once read all the published psychology books by one particular examiner to discover his particular fields of interest. This was on the assumption that, having set the paper previously, he would be doing so again and that his choice of questions would reflect his interests. When the paper was issued to me in the examination hall, I found that it had been set by an entirely different examiner. So a far better counsel to the candidate than that of trying to spot the question is: *Know your subject well and be prepared for anything.*

Examiners themselves are aware that some candidates try to spot the questions and that some teachers encourage their students in this practice. So they are forced to do a little 'spotting' of their own, trying to distinguish the candidate who has 'crammed' from the one who has really studied the syllabus. So even if you succeed in identifying the topic of a question, the question itself may have been given some original twist which will make your prepared answer next to useless.

Go into the exam room with the right tools and enough of them. For instance, if you need a sharp-pointed pencil, take two, so that in case one breaks you don't have to lose time sharpening it. Take something to sharpen it with anyway — just in case the other one breaks. Make sure that you have plenty of ink and a good pen — or two good pens in case one packs up before the examination is over.

Handwriting is important in exams and papers that are difficult to read prejudice a candidate's chances of success. An experiment by Dennis Briggs, a staff tutor with the Open University, showed that examiners marked quite differently identical copies of the same CSE language-paper essay written in different handwritings. So remember that poor writing may turn a potential pass into a failure.

If you can't see the clock, make sure that your watch is wound, showing the right time and keeping good time. Take your glasses and a handkerchief with you, if you are likely to need them. Remember to go to the toilet before the examination starts. If you are a girl, calculate whether your period is going to coincide with your examination. If you do not feel at your best at such times, it may be advisable to consult your doctor. Don't spoil your chances by lack of attenton to some trivial detail that may become vitally important if neglected.

I wish you every success in your forthcoming examination, which I am sure you now look forward to tackling with confidence. I know you will succeed if you remember to apply the hints offered above. It would interest me very much to learn your examination result when it is announced. You are cordially invited to write to me about it care of my publishers.

6.

How to Forget

No discussion on how to remember would be complete without some reference to how to forget. It will be the purpose of the present chapter to make good this omission.

Indeed to some unhappy and disappointed people forgetting may be more important than remembering. They may have undergone upsetting experiences which they would prefer to put behind them but do not seem able to do.

'Memory has its important and proportionate place in the scale of mental life,' writes Dr Henry Knight Miller in an essay on 'The Ministry of Forgetfulness' (*Life Triumphant*, p. 137). 'So has "forgettery." We need to learn the fine art of relegating into the mental discard life's sordidness, griefs, errors, failures and disappointments . . . The capacity to forget is an essential prerequisite for happiness. You cannot be happy while constantly pursued by haunting memories of past transgressions, errors and failures.'[104]

Just as it is possible to deduce practical hints on remembering from knowing what causes forgetting, the same information can yield us practical help in forgetting what we wish not to remember.

The type of experience which people would like to be able to forget is illustrated by the following report. 'I was a cook in a firm's canteen. A group of employees presented a petition to the manageress that the meals were not satisfactory. This was a great shock to me. I had received no complaints direct. The humiliation is for ever tormenting me. Can you tell me how to forget this unpleasant memory?'

What we have learned about the causes of forgetting may be briefly summarized as follows:

1.   We forget because the experience makes a weak impression.

2. We forget because of the lapse of time.
3. We forget because we did or thought something else afterwards or beforehand.
4. We forget because we repress certain memories.

1. Weak Impression

The first principle is that we forget because the impression is a weak one. Often, of course, the experiences that prove difficult to forget do so for the very reason that they have left a strong impression. They are often experiences that have been strongly charged with unpleasant emotions. But even experiences of this kind can be weakened in their effect, if dealt with at the time when they occur.

We have seen that when an experience occurs it leaves a physical trace in the brain structure. This physical trace takes a certain time to 'settle' before it becomes firmly embedded in the mind. During this process of 'consolidation', as it is called, the memory trace is subject to interference and may even be erased completely.

If the experience is denied this settling-down period by immediate introduction of fresh experiences, it fails to consolidate or to make a proper impression. The result is that its effect upon the mind is considerably reduced.

'You can only recall an impression,' writes Dr Miller, 'when you are attending to it. If you refuse to attend to it as it knocks at the door of consciousness and demands attention, it will be relegated, temporarily at least, into the realm of forgetfulness.'

Bergson suggested that the function of the brain and nervous system is in the main eliminative — to protect us from being overwhelmed and confused by shutting out most of what we should otherwise remember at any moment, and leaving only what is likely to be useful.

It may be that the time required for the brain to consolidate memories serves this eliminative function. At any rate, for a few minutes after a memory trace is formed it is easily disturbed; if left undisturbed it 'hardens' or consolidates and can resist interference. We shall have more to say about this topic and its practical application to the problem of forgetting later on in this chapter.

2. Disuse

The second principle is that we forget because of the lapse of time. The fact that an impression has consolidated does not mean that it will not fade eventually. Although this natural process of forgetting is slow and passive, it can still be useful to the person who wishes to erase an unpleasant memory.

It means, in fact, that such a person has time on his side. For example, a man said: 'I saw the body of a man who had been knocked down and killed in a road accident. The thought of this incident has kept on coming back to my mind in spite of my efforts to forget it. I want to get rid of this unwanted memory, although I am pleased to say that *it is somewhat decreasing day by day.*'

'As we look back over the years,' reflects Dr Miller, 'the friendly hand of time tends to place in proper perspective those experiences which, when we were passing through them, seemed unbearable. Now they add just a touch of colour to the picture life paints and are needed to give the proper and complete background.'

3. Interference

Nevertheless, one should not rely purely and simply upon the passing of the years to mend a broken heart. Besides the slow and passive method one should make use of a quick and active method. The difference between the two may be likened to a wound which is left undressed and one which receives medical attention. The healing power of nature will clear up the former in time. But the latter will heal more promptly and cleanly.

We have seen that it is not so much time itself that counts as the use that we make of it. Of course, the two are really inseparable, since no one can live in a mental or social vacuum, nor have experiences without growing older. We should, however, seek other experiences which will help us to forget the unpleasant experience. The effectiveness of this remedy depends upon four conditions:

(a) *The greater the similarity of needs involved in the unpleasant experience and what we do or think afterwards, the easier we shall forget the former.* For example, the best cure for a broken love affair is a new one that is successful. Try moving around a bit, and see what it does for you. There are plenty of people with whom you can fall in love and satisfy your emotional needs.

(b) *The more active we are in the interval, the more likely we are to forget.* This means that the more impressions we can superimpose on an unpleasant one, the better our chances of forgetting it. It underlines the value of keeping yourself busy after you have undergone something that has upset you.

When something happens which you want to forget, lose no time in obliterating it with other impressions. Don't seclude yourself and brood over the event. Don't fall a victim to feeling sorry for yourself. Resist the inclination to indulge in self-pity. Instead, get out and do things. Get among new people, and see new faces, new scenes. Avoid going to the places which in your mind are associated with the broken romance. A change of environment is what the doctor orders in such a situation.

(c) *The less vivid the effect of the original impression, the less likely are we to remember it and the more will other activities help us still further to forget it.* Of course, this is not always easy to arrange. We cannot always control the intensity of the disappointing experiences that we undergo. However, where we can it is as well to do so.

(d) *There is more forgetting during waking activity than during sleep.* For example, suppose you came home one evening and found a letter from your beloved telling you that she intended to marry another man. If you decided to sleep on the problem, you would give the memory a better chance to consolidate than if you went out and saw an exciting film.

The further waking activity of watching the film would help you to forget your disappointment better than if you went to bed and slept, and much better than if you went to bed and lay awake turning the problem over and over in your mind.

Of course, this is something which is easier to preach than to practise. You have to weigh up, however, the pros and cons of the matter. You have to put in the balance the trouble of making yourself do something active against the chance of forgetting something which, unless forgotten, will make you miserable.

We also forget an event because of what we did or thought *before* it happened. This is an argument in favour of doing or thinking at all times positive and constructive things which will form a kind of mental reserve pool upon which we can draw for consolation in time of need or distress. The man or woman who in later years can look back upon a life of solid achievement, having contributed something to the world, can stand unshaken when the tempests of vicissitude rage around him. To be able to feel that one may have left the world just a little better for his having lived in it is bound to provide a source of strength buttressing one against the rude shocks of existence.

4. Repression

Although repression has no practical application to the problem of how to forget, there is a closely allied mental process which has the advantages of repression without its disadvantages. Some people have the knack of being able to push an undesirable memory to the back of their minds. Although they think about it occasionally, it does not keep on forcing itself on their attention. This is known as suppression. For those who are capable of it suppression offers a practical way of disposing of an unwanted memory — at least temporarily.

The teaching of psychology has sufficiently emphasized the evil effects of repression, which is responsible for the production of much mental and bodily sickness of various kinds. Suppression, therefore, should not be confused with repression. Whereas repression means that one refuses to acknowledge a thought or memory, suppression amounts to acknowledging and controlling it, because by so doing a person realizes that he will favour his chances of eventual happiness and success.

When we suppress we are aware both of what we are suppressing and of the fact that we are suppressing; in repression, on the other hand, we are no longer aware of what is repressed, nor are we aware of the process by which we do the repressing.

To summarize, then, we can encourage the forgetting of an unpleasant experience if we:

1. Introduce fresh experiences which prevent the unwanted memory from 'settling down'.
2. Rely upon the healing power of time.
3. Satisfy in another way the need which the unpleasant memory has frustrated.
4. Seek fresh interests or a change of environment.
5. Remember that waking activity helps us to forget better than 'sleeping on it'.

6. Build up throughout life a reserve stock of pleasant experiences upon which we can look back when things go against us.
7. Push the unpleasant experience to the back of our minds.

7.

Summary of Practical Hints

1. What is Memory?

Remembering is the activity of attending to present ideas which are determined by past experiences. A past event which we are able to revive as a present experience leaves a physiological change in the brain structure called a memory trace.

Pure memory is the activity of attending to a particular experience, as, for example, when I remember what I ate for my Christmas dinner last year. Habit memory is the knowledge acquired by experience as distinct from the particular experiences of acquiring it.

Memory differs from both imagination and thinking. The function of images in memory is to represent past experiences. In imagination the images relate to what is thought of as occurring in the future. Past experience is made use of both in memory and in thinking, but whereas memory is a direct use of what has been learned, thinking is an indirect use. Remembering is performing a previously learned act, while thinking is doing something partly original.

Those who have difficulty in forming mental images can derive encouragement from two sources. One is that mental imagery doesn't have to be all that vivid to be effective as a memory aid. The other is that verbal memory (thinking with words) can be used instead of mental pictures.

If you cannot form mental pictures at all, there are also two things you can do. One is to rely on verbal memory or thinking. And you may be able to use images based on senses other than sight, e.g. auditory (hearing), tactile (touch), olfactory (smell), even gustatory (taste).

It does not follow that the more intelligent a person is, the better his memory is bound to be. Nor can it be said that the less intelligent he is, the worse his memory. Success in remembering depends upon interest, attention, and persistence as well as intelligence.

2. Why Do We Forget?

You read and reread a chapter in a book, yet a few minutes afterwards you cannot relate one word of what you have read. This is usually caused by lack of attention, so that the experience does not make a proper impression upon us.

Forgetting is also due to the lapse of time between an experience and the attempt to recall it. As a result of the normal metabolic processes of the brain a memory trace tends to face or decay with the passage of time, unless we renew it by repeating the experience which gave rise to it. Much of what we learn is forgotten almost as soon as we have learned it. Forgetting proceeds most rapidly immediately after learning but less rapidly as the interval increases.

Changes occurring in the brain with the passing of time also lead to things being 'remembered' that never occurred or that occurred differently from the way they are remembered. (Distortion.)

The view that the lapse of time alone accounts for the decay of a memory trace is too simple. For a few minutes after a memory trace is formed it is easily disturbed. If left undisturbed, the trace hardens or consolidates and can resist interference. During the process of consolidation, however, the memory trace is still susceptible to a type of interference known as retroactive inhibition from material which is learned subsequently (and also, as we shall see later, from material which has been learned before).

This has led to the formulation of the view that we forget because we do or think something else afterwards. The principle of retroactive inhibition states that the trace left behind by an earlier activity is impaired by a later one.

This means that we tend to forget a certain thing not simply because it is a week ago since we learned it, but because we have since learned other things the memory traces of which have interfered with the memory trace of the original thing. The more active we are in the interval, the more likely we are to forget. The better we learn the original task, the more likely we are to remember it in spite of interpolated activities.

As we noted in Chapter 3, there are certain conditions under which retroactive inhibition operates. One of these is that the greatest loss of retention occurs by shifting directly to material of a very similar kind. The more a later experience resembles an earlier one, the more likely are we to forget the latter. But a point is eventually reached when the similarity is close enough to assist the remembering of the original material rather than interfere with it.

If waking activity interferes with recall, we should remember better after sleep, when less activity has intervened. You do, in fact, forget less when asleep than when awake. You lose a little during the first hour or two of sleep, but after that you forget very little more during the night. For example, a person who read a story before going to sleep could remember many details when he was awakened. When he remained awake after reading the story, he forgot more of the details.

The principle of proactive inhibition states that work which *precedes* learning also tends to interfere with the retention of the learned material. What happened before an experience causes us to forget it as well as what happened afterwards.

There is also a process of unconscious forgetting of painful memories known as repression. Such memories may not be recalled because of the sense of anxiety or guilt which they would provoke if they were. We tend to remember events which give us satisfaction and to forget those which are annoying to us. We more easily forget an experience which conflicts with our comfort and self-esteem than one which does not. The tendency of a memory to become repressed varies directly with the anguish which accompanies it.

Senility, too, is a cause of forgetting, although as it cannot be eliminated we are not concerned with it in this book. Some people approaching old age can barely remember the events of the day, although their memory for events of the distant past and childhood may be unimpaired. This type of forgetting occurs through the organic changes taking place in the brain and nervous system with the passing years.

A poor memory is caused, then, by the memory trace not having much energy to begin with, by not being recharged or fading with the laspe of time, and by losing its energy to other memory traces. There is also a form of forgetting, known as repression, caused by resistance or opposition from something else in the mind to the recall of a painful memory.

Yet other causes are shock and drugs. Shock is of two kinds — that resulting from an intense emotional experience and that resulting from psychiatric treatment for nervous or mental illness. Drugs, taken with or without medical justification, can hamper remembering. Particularly dangerous is marijuana or pot, which damages the brain because it contains substances soluble in the brain's fat. Chronic heavy smoking could also impair the memory although as yet there is no evidence to support this view.

The main causes of forgetting may thus be briefly summarized as follows:

1. We forget an experience because it makes a weak impression on us.
2. We forget an experience because we don't refresh our memory of it.
3. We forget an experience because other experiences interfere with it.
4. We forget an experience because it creates a conflict between the wish to remember it and the wish not to remember it.
5. We forget because the brain is affected by the physiological changes accompanying old age, shock, the use of drugs, and possibly the use of tobacco.

3. How Can We Remember?

The first cause of a poor memory is that an experience makes a weak impression on us. To secure a strong impression it is necessary to concentrate on what we wish to remember.

Lack of concentration is caused by the habit of day-dreaming, lack of interest in the subject, too little or too much muscular tension, and worry or emotional conflict, which distracts attention from what we are doing.

Therefore, we can acquire the habit of concentration if we:

1. Bring our mind back every time it wanders to other things.
2. Strengthen our interest in the subject by means of autosuggestion.
3. Lightly brace ourselves (but not too much) as we work.
4. Try to deal with the emotional problems that distract our attention.

The second cause is that we allow time to elapse without refreshing our memory. This cause can be removed by repeating whatever it is we wish to remember. The more frequently a thing is repeated, the more likely it is to be remembered.

To be most effective in refreshing our memory repetition depends upon certain conditions, which may be stated in the form of the following practical rules:

1. Always make an effort to understand the material which you are repeating.
2. A few minutes' repetition every day is better than a greater amount of repetition less often.
3. A better method of repetition than reading and rereading is to read and then try to recall what has been read.
4. Do not repeat what you wish to remember until you barely know it, but until you know it really well.
5. It is better to repeat the material as a whole than to break it up into parts and repeat each part separately.
6. Use autosuggestion to acquire confidence in your ability to remember what you repeat.
7. Repeat your work at the same table or desk in the same room with your books arranged in the same way.
8. Break off your repetition before you come to a natural division of the subject-matter, for if you are working without emotional stress you will remember an uncompleted task better than a completed one. On the other hand, if you are more interested in what the study can do for you than in the study itself, it may be better to complete the task, for you will remember a completed task better than an uncompleted one.
9. Try to arrange that what you wish to learn contrasts in some way with the background against which you are studying it.

The third cause of forgetting is that the memory traces of other experiences interfere with the memory trace of the experience we wish to remember. This interference is less active during sleep than during waking hours. It is less active between different types of material than between similar types. It concerns what we do before an experience as well as what we do afterwards.

The practical application of these principles to the problem of overcoming retroactive and proactive inhibition is as follows:

1. Go to bed after studying in the evening rather than take up further waking activity.
2. Revise the material in the morning before the activity of the day makes you forget too much of it.
3. Avoid other mental work, especially of a similar kind, in the event that you cannot go to bed after studying.
4. Change to a different form of learning in the event that one period of study must be followed by another.
5. Take a brief rest before studying a lesson rather than engage in other mental activity, especially similar mental activity.
6. Endeavour to ensure that it is a different type of study if one period of study must be immediately followed by another.

The fourth cause of forgetting is repression. There are various ways in which a repression can be undone, thus helping us to remember better.

1. We can rely upon the repressed memory occurring to us spontaneously.
2. We can run through the alphabet until we come to a letter associated with the repressed memory.
3. We can run through consecutive numbers, starting with 0, until we come to one which reminds us of the forgotten number.
4. We can recall a repressed thought or memory by interpreting a dream which embodies it.
5. We can wait to be reminded of the repressed memory by some happening during the course of the day.
6. We can often remember something by 'sleeping on it'. If we take a problem to bed with us, we may find that in the morning we remember how to solve it.
7. We can repeat or imagine ourselves repeating the situation in which we first experienced what we want to recall.
8. We can make use of free association, writing down whatever thoughts occur to us until we recall the repressed memory.
9. We should also make use of any available associations in committing something to memory. Two ideas may be associated

if they resemble or contrast with each other, or if they simply occur together.

4. How Can We Use Mnemonics in Learning?

Mnemonics, once despised by academic psychologists, have now come into their own, thanks to serious research which has validated their usefulness. Simple mnemonics represent a way of programming the human computer. They are of several types, involving the use of: initial letters, acronyms, rhyming jingles, associations, digits represented by words, and word-play. Those that codify the material in a shortened form, e.g., acronyms, are *reductive*; those that enlarge upon it, e.g., rhyming mnemonics, are *elaborative*.

It is an interesting and useful exercise to devise your own mnemonics. Chapter 4 gives numerous examples illustrating how this can be done. For example, the Morse code can be learned by devising mnemonic words in which vowels represent dots and consonants dashes.

Place memory employs mental pictures which associate items to be learned with places (loci) in a building or on a street. It enables you to recall any point at random, irrespective of its position in the prememorized series of loci. So it is suitable for memorizing items where you want to recall a particular one without going through the whole series from the beginning every time. For this purpose it is best to use places which you are thoroughly familiar with and which you can readily visualize in your mind's eye.

Words can also be employed as loci in the place-memory method. They can be selected to rhyme with the cardinal numbers from 1 to 12, e.g., gun, shoe, tree, door, hive, sticks, heaven, gate, wine, pen, Devon, delve. Turned into mental images, these can be used to form associations with a list of twelve or fewer items to be learned. If your material contains more than twelve items, add each further item to one of the mental images already formed.

Letters, too, can be used as places, e.g., the letters of the Latin cryptogram or word square:

```
R O T A S
O P E R A
T E N E T
A R E P O
S A T O R
```

In this case, associate each point in the material to be recalled with one of the above letters. State the point in the form of a sentence that begins with the letter you want to associate it with.

The letters spelling the name of a topic can be used in this way. *Link each letter to one point in your material by stating the point in the form of a sentence beginning with that letter.*

To recall the material, carry out the following steps:

1. Hold in mind the letter-place word, phrase, or sentence related to your subject-matter.
2. Mentally work through the letters which spell it, reviving the points which you have associated with them. Each letter will remind you of a word that begins with that letter, and each word is the first word of a statement embodying the point to be recalled.
3. This recall provides you with the facts which you need to answer a question on that subject, whether written or oral.

5. How Can We Pass Exams?

Chapter 5 brings out the following points on the technique of passing exams:

1. Cultivate a keen *interest* in your subject by thinking about your reasons for studying it, by relating the material to your own life, and by visualizing yourself achieving your purpose.
2. Make *notes* on the content of what you read or hear. Either write a summary in continuous prose or develop an outline with lettered and/or numbered headings and subheadings. Notice how both methods are used in this summary chapter.
3. When *learning notes*:

    (a) Make an effort to understand the material.
    (b) Study a little at a time at fairly frequent intervals rather than for long stretches at less frequent intervals.
    (c) Instead of reading and rereading, read and then try to recall. Use the P-V formula:
    Preview your material to get a general idea of what it is about.
    Question yourself on points which you want your reading to answer.
    Read and make sure that you understand.

Summarize the material in either or both of the note forms suggested under (2) above.

Test yourself on it.

Use what you have learned.

Visualize the ideas in your mind's eye.

(d) Overlearn your material, i.e., until you know it really well rather than just barely.

(e) If you are interested in the subject-matter itself, break off before you get to one of its natural divisions. If you are interested in what it can do for you, complete the section or chapter before breaking off.

(f) Revise as soon as possible after learning.

(g) Use the same study place each time.

(h) Lightly brace yourself (but not too much) as you work.

(i) Tell yourself that you can succeed.

(j) Practise answering questions set in previous papers.

4. *Revise* during your course as well as at the end of it.

5. *Confront the paper* with the right mental attitude of confidence. Read it carefully. Follow the examiner's instructions. Say to yourself: 'What is he asking for?' Having decided, give it to him. Present your answers methodically, legibly, clearly, and relevantly. Keep an eye on the clock. Leave yourself a little time at the end.

6. Answer *essay-type exams* from a course outline carried in your head. Select the headings and material for your answer, organizing them intelligently and systematically. Write concisely. Keep your outline flexible enough to allow the inclusion of ideas that occur to you while you are writing. If you run short of time, put down the rest of your ideas in summary form. Then press on with the next question.

7. Distinguish among the various *terms* that examiners are fond of, e.g., comment, criticize, explain, etc. (See pages 143-47 for definitions and examples.)

8. Use *correct grammar, spelling, and punctuation*. In particular, don't misspell a word which actually appears in the paper.

9. Pay particular attention to the *opening and closing paragraphs* of your answer.

10. See if you can *use one part of the paper to help you in answering another*.
11. *Know your subject well and be prepared for anything*.
12. Make sure that you have the right *tools* with you in the examination room.

6. How Can We Forget?

A study of the four causes of forgetting yields practical hints on how to forget as well as on how to remember. These practical hints may be briefly summarized as follows:

1. Weaken the impression left by a disturbing emotional experience by turning your attention to fresh experiences as soon as possible after it has occurred.

2. Rely upon the power of time to heal the wounds of the soul. The person who wishes to forget an unpleasant experience has time on his side.

3. Find other interests that will help to obliterate the disappointments of the past. Seek other experiences that will erase the memory of the previous unpleasant experience. The greater the similarity of needs involved, the easier we shall forget the disappointment. The best cure for a broken love affair is a new one that is successful.

    Keep yourself busy after you have undergone something likely to upset you. Avoid going to the places which in your mind are associated with the broken romance. Don't go to bed and sleep immediately after a disappointing experience, but get out and get a change of scene to take your mind off the problem.

4. Build up throughout life a reserve stock of pleasant experiences upon which you can look back when things go against you.

5. Avoid expecting to banish unpleasant memories by 'repressing' them, i.e., by denying to yourself that they ever occurred. This method of forgetting has no practical application to the problem, because it is not under the conscious control of the will but occurs without our being aware of it, and because unless what is repressed is sublimated or worked off indirectly, it leads to the appearance of nervous symptoms. But what you shouldn't repress you may be able to suppress. That is, you may be able to push it more or less to the back of your mind so that it is not bothering you all the time.

'Refresh Your Memory' Quiz

Check each statement by ringing TRUE *or* FALSE *in pencil*

1. Past experiences are determined by present ideas.   TRUE/FALSE
2. Past events leave a memory trace in the brain.   TRUE/FALSE
3. Pure memory means attending to a particular past experience.   TRUE/FALSE
4. Habit memory is the knowledge acquired by experience.   TRUE/FALSE
5. Past experiences are represented in memory by images.   TRUE/FALSE
6. An experience makes a weak impression on us unless we attend to it properly.   TRUE/FALSE
7. A memory trace is normally strengthened by the passage of time.   TRUE/FALSE
8. Little of what we learn is forgotten as soon as we have learned it.   TRUE/FALSE
9. When we 'remember' things that never occurred this is called 'distortion'.   TRUE/FALSE
10. The lapse of time alone accounts for the decay of a memory trace.   TRUE/FALSE
11. If left undisturbed a trace hardens or consolidates.   TRUE/FALSE
12. Doing or thinking something else afterwards does not make us forget.   TRUE/FALSE
13. The better we learn something the less we are likely to forget it.   TRUE/FALSE
14. The more a later experience resembles an earlier one, the more likely are we to forget the latter.   TRUE/FALSE
15. What we learn is forgotten faster while we are asleep than while we are awake.   TRUE/FALSE
16. A topic swotted up before going to bed stays in our mind the following morning.   TRUE/FALSE
17. Work which precedes learning tends to interfere with the remembering of learned material.   TRUE/FALSE
18. The forgetting of pleasant memories is known as repression.   TRUE/FALSE

19. Something which conflicts with our self-esteem is forgotten slower than something which doesn't. TRUE/FALSE

20. Senility is never a cause of forgetting. TRUE/FALSE

21. Organic changes take place in the brain as we grow older. TRUE/FALSE

22. We get a strong impression of what we wish to remember if we concentrate on it. TRUE/FALSE

23. Lack of concentration is caused by day-dreaming. TRUE/FALSE

24. We can concentrate on a subject better if we are not interested in it. TRUE/FALSE

25. Too little or too much muscular tension causes lack of concentration. TRUE/FALSE

26. Worry distracts our attention from what we are doing. TRUE/FALSE

27. Autosuggestion can be used to strengthen our interest in a subject. TRUE/FALSE

28. To concentrate better we should tense ourselves strongly as we work. TRUE/FALSE

29. We should repeat whatever we wish to remember. TRUE/FALSE

30. The less often it is repeated the better it is remembered. TRUE/FALSE

31. The better you understand something the better you can remember it. TRUE/FALSE

32. 'Lots but seldom' is a better study rule than 'little but often'. TRUE/FALSE

33. Reading and rereading is the best method of study. TRUE/FALSE

34. Something you wish to remember should be repeated only until you barely know it. TRUE/FALSE

35. It is better to repeat your material as a whole than to break it up into parts. TRUE/FALSE

36. Confidence in your ability to remember can be acquired by means of autosuggestion. TRUE/FALSE

37. It is better to move about from room to room than always to study in the same place. TRUE/FALSE

38. When we are working under emotional stress an uncompleted task is remembered better than a completed one.   TRUE/FALSE

39. An item which blends with its background is better remembered than one which contrasts with it.   TRUE/FALSE

40. Other memory traces do not interfere with the memory trace we wish to remember.   TRUE/FALSE

41. It is better to take up further waking activity than to go to bed after studying in the evening.   TRUE/FALSE

42. The material we have learned in the evening should be revised the following morning.   TRUE/FALSE

43. If one study period is immediately followed by another it should if possible be a different subject.   TRUE/FALSE

44. A repressed memory can occur to us spontaneously.   TRUE/FALSE

45. A repressed memory can be recalled by interpreting a dream.   TRUE/FALSE

46. A problem can be solved by 'sleeping on it'.   TRUE/FALSE

47. Free association means writing down whatever thoughts come into our head.   TRUE/FALSE

48. Two ideas may be associated if they resemble each other.   TRUE/FALSE

49. Two ideas may be associated if they contrast with each other.   TRUE/FALSE

50. Two ideas may be associated if they have occurred together.   TRUE/FALSE

51. To take a more active part in learning is a help in remembering.   TRUE/FALSE

52. To forget turn your attention to fresh experiences.   TRUE/FALSE

53. We can rely upon the power of time to help us to forget.   TRUE/FALSE

54. The best cure for a broken love affair is a new successful one.   TRUE/FALSE

55. A reserve stock of unpleasant experiences is a source of comfort in troubled times.   TRUE/FALSE

56. Repression is under the control of our will.   TRUE/FALSE

57. Repression is a cause of nervous symptoms. TRUE/FALSE
58. Suppression means pushing something to the back of your mind. TRUE/FALSE
59. Academic psychologists used to sneer at mnemonic devices. TRUE/FALSE
60. Artificial associations are the only way of connecting disconnected facts. TRUE/FALSE
61. Simple mnemonics are one method of programming the human computer. TRUE/FALSE
62. There is only one type of simple mnemonic device. TRUE/FALSE
63. Place memory is probably the oldest memory system known to man. TRUE/FALSE
64. Place memory does not require you to be familiar with the places you use. TRUE/FALSE
65. Words and letters can be employed instead of images of places. TRUE/FALSE
66. In the letter-place method each letter is linked to one point in the material. TRUE/FALSE
67. An examiner never gives away any information in setting a question. TRUE/FALSE
68. A basic essential to passing an exam is a keen interest in the subject. TRUE/FALSE
69. Jedediah Buxton was an inveterate note-taker. TRUE/FALSE
70. Reading and rereading your material is the best way of learning it. TRUE/FALSE
71. Revision is best deferred until the end of your course. TRUE/FALSE
72. Revision can take the form of applying the material to practical situations. TRUE/FALSE
73. A JMB report said: 'Candidates were intent on answering the question rather than regurgitating information'. TRUE/FALSE
74. You can get the examiner on your side by making your answer easy to read. TRUE/FALSE
75. 'Answer either . . . or . . .' implies that you will score extra marks by answering both questions. TRUE/FALSE

76. 'Criticize' means 'Give reasons that account for'.   TRUE/FALSE
77. 'Outline' means the same as 'Summarize'.   TRUE/FALSE
78. Sometimes one part of an exam paper can supply
      the answer to another.   TRUE/FALSE
79. Trying to 'spot' questions is a chancy procedure.   TRUE/FALSE
80. Handwriting is important in exams.   TRUE/FALSE

Key to 'Refresh Your Memory' Quiz

1, 7, 8, 10, 12, 15, 18-20, 24, 28, 30, 32-34, 37-41, 55, 56, 62, 64,
67, 69-71, 73, 75 and 76 are FALSE; the rest are TRUE. The above
items should read as follows:

1. Present ideas are determined by past experiences.
7. A memory trace is normally weakened by the passage of time.
8. Much of what we learn is forgotten as soon as we have learned it.
10. The lapse of time alone does not account for the decay of a memory
    trace.
12. Doing or thinking something else afterwards makes us forget.
15. What we learn is forgotten slower while we are asleep than while
    we are awake.
18. The forgetting of unpleasant memories is known as repression.
19. Something which conflicts with our self-esteem is forgotten faster
    than something which doesn't.
20. Senility is a cause of forgetting of recent events.
24. We can concentrate on a subject better if we are interested in it.
28. To concentrate better we should not tense ourselves too much as
    we work.
30. The more often it is repeated the better it is remembered.
32. 'Little but often' is a better study rule than 'lots but seldom'.
33. Reading and rereading is not the best method of study; a better
    method is to read and then try to recall what has been read.
34. Something you wish to remember should be repeated until you
    know it really well.
37. It is better to study in the same place than to move about from room
    to room.
38. When we are working under emotional stress a completed task is
    remembered better than an uncompleted one; OR When we are

working without emotional stress an uncompleted task is remembered better than a completed one.

39. An item which contrasts with its background is better remembered than one which blends with it.

40. Other memory traces interfere with the memory trace we wish to remember.

41. It is better to go to bed after studying in the evening than to take up further waking activity.

55. A reserve stock of pleasant experiences is a source of comfort in troubled times.

56. Repression is not under the conscious control of the will.

62. There are several types of simple mnemonic devices.

64. Place memory works best if you use places that you are familiar with.

67. An examiner gives away the information that the question deals with a particular topic.

69. Jedediah Buxton never learned to write.

70. The use of the P-V formula is a better way than reading and rereading.

71. Revision should be done during the course as well as at the end of it.

73. The report said: 'Too many candidates were determined to regurgitate information rather than to answer the question.'

75. 'Answer either . . . or . . .' implies that both questions carry equal marks and you can score full marks by answering only one.

76. 'Criticize' means 'Express an opinion about'. To give reasons that account for something is to *explain* it.

Appendix

How to Read Faster

What is read and understood quickly is remembered at least as well as what is read and understood slowly and may be remembered better. With quicker reading, says Harry Bayley, 'the amount of the material which is remembered after one reading is at least as much, and generally more, than that remembered after a slow reading . . . You can read twice as fast and remember just as much.' Discussing the view that better understanding comes from reading more slowly and carefully, he comments that this is 'Excellent advice for the beginner, but an impediment to the efficient.'[105]

The average reader can read between two hundred and three hundred words per minute. A slow reader reads between a hundred and two hundred words per minute, while a fast reader may read up to four hundred words per minute.

In reading a line the eyes make several jumps. This is because they are reading separate words or phrases. A fast reader makes three or four jumps per line on the average. This means that he reads three or four words at a time. A slow reader may make a dozen or more jumps. This is because he reads each word separately and looks back at words already read.

To train yourself to read faster you should practise making fewer eye movements. Fix your eyes on the centre of each line, and then let them run down the page instead of across it. Try not to say the words to yourself, and don't look back at what you have already read. Begin with simple material such as short stories and other light literature. As your reading rate improves, choose more difficult material.

'Improved speed in my reading,' said Mr R. D., 'came to me when I timed myself on short articles, essays and other such brief items. The sense of speeding up was quickly acquired and easily carried over from the shorter work to book-length reading.'

If you want to, you can cut a slit in a postcard wide enough and high enough to expose one full line at a time. By sliding it down the page as you read you can force yourself to read at a faster pace. This idea is adapted from a training film in which a few words are illuminated at a time, beginning at 180 words per minute and working up to 570 words per minute.

To aid this practice of fast reading two psychologists, Dr Goodwin Watson and Dr Theodore Newcomb, have formulated five simple rules.

1. Eliminate whispering, pointing and movements of the lips, head and hands as you read. Such movements tend to slow up your reading and distract the mind from its effort to understand what you read.
2. Practise relaxation of your muscles. Sit down to read in an easy chair. Make sure that you are physically comfortable.
3. Try to read phrases, sentences, or even paragraphs rather than single words.
4. Try not to let your mind wander. If you find yourself thinking of something else, write down a note about it to be taken up later. See pages 61-73 of this book about how to concentrate.
5. Try to anticipate the argument the author is setting forth. Ask yourself whether he is developing his ideas on the lines you would expect.

Get a general idea of what you are going to read before you begin to read it. You can learn quite a lot about a book from the dust-jacket and from reviews published in newspapers and literary periodicals. The table of contents, the preface, the author's own summaries of his arguments, and the index also give a lot of information. One can get the hang of the subject by mastering the headings and subheadings. If you want to get a firm grasp of a book's contents in the least possible time, you can obtain help from all these sources.

Do not attempt to read too much all at once at the increased rate. If you keep on for a long time, fatigue will tend to set in and you will revert to your slower rate of reading. That is why short practice periods are desirable at the start. When the faster rate becomes habitual, however, it is no more tiring than a slower rate.

The following report will be of interest at this point.

'My eyes are centred on the middle word in each line,' said a man who followed this method of reading, 'and instead of moving from left to right, they travel straight down the centre of the page, taking in a line at time. I learned to do it when I was a student, and it saves me hours every week spent on reading.'

Understanding is, of course, just as important as speed. It may be asked what sense there is in reading fast if a person does not understand what he reads. The answer is that it is better to read what one does not understand rapidly than to read it slowly. The sooner one discovers that one does not understand it, the sooner one can go over it again or go on to another book that explains it better.

Therefore, to see whether you have gathered ideas and information from rapid reading, it is as well to close the book from time to time and jot down what you have read or run over it in your mind. Read for five or ten minutes and then stop to think about what you have read. If something the author has said has confused you or seems contrary to fact, go back and read the passage over again, thinking about the doubtful point.

A student said: 'My experience is that speedier reading is reading with greater understanding because you have to keep alert to maintain the speed and this wide-awakeness means more attention to the subject-matter. I find that I take away practically as much from a speedy reading as from a leisurely one.'

A book can also be read rapidly by 'skimming' through it. If you know what not to read, you can pick out the more important parts, just casting your eye over the less important ones. Some things need plenty of concentration, while others call for less of it. It is wise to adjust your method to the material. Learn the art of judicious skipping. Discriminate between what is and what is not worth your attention.

Theodore Roosevelt was once lent a book by a diplomat at a reception. At the close of the evening he handed the book back with a brief comment. The diplomat was offended because he thought that the President had not read the book. Roosevelt thereupon led him to his study, where he discussed the book's contents with him. The President was a rapid reader and had slipped away from his guests to master the book.

Learning more words also helps one to read faster. 'By constantly reading,' said Mrs B. G., 'I have become much more familiar with words and their meanings. Having a better knowledge of words, I can read with greater speed than before.'

Pay attention, too, to your eyesight. Have your eyes tested and, if necessary, have glasses fitted. Defects of sight are obstacles to rapid reading. Be sure that there is enough light but avoid glare on the page. Once the eyes become tired reading is slower and poorer.

If you want to put into effect the recommendations offered above, first of all measure your normal reading speed. You can do this by timing yourself as you read the following passage, which contains two hundred words. Read at the comfortable rate which you adopt every day, being careful to take in the meaning of what you read.

Start timing yourself now. To remember a thing it is necessary to pay attention to it. Much impaired memory is really impaired concentration. We do not remember a thing because our attention is distracted from it by something else. Besides repeating it and so establishing it firmly it is necessary to be interested in it. Remembering it is also assisted if we associate or link it up in the mind with something which is already there. The conditions upon which association depends are: similarity, contrast and contiguity. We can associate two things if they resemble each other. For example, we can associate the Italian word *tutto* with the French word *tout*. We can associate by contrast. An English motorist who takes his car to the Continent remembers to drive on the right side of the road by contrast with the left side on which he drives in England. Association also occurs by contiguity. Two things may be associated with each other because they have occurred together in space, e.g., apples and custard, or time, e.g., Christmas and carols, or both, e.g., Hiroshima and the atomic bomb. These four points — Attention, Repetition, Interest and Association — may be remembered by means of the mnemonic word A R I A. *Stop timing yourself now.*

You can work out your normal reading speed from the following table:

Time in seconds	Reading speed in words per minute
80	150
75	160
70	171
65	185
60	200

Time in seconds	Reading speed in words per minute
55	218
50	240
45	267
40	300
35	343

If your reading speed is not shown above you can work it out by dividing 12,000 by the number of seconds you took to read the piece.

Now read the following passage, which contains one hundred words. This time read as fast as you can without loss of comprehension. Deliberately force yourself to read at a faster pace than you normally do. Again time yourself.

Start timing yourself now. Most people in reading fixate their attention on the left of the page and let the eyes (sometimes the head as well) move across to the right. To speed up your rate fix your attention on the centre of the page and let the eyes move downwards, taking in a line at a time. Comprehension improves as speed improves, or it can be improved separately. This is done by reading a section and then, having closed the book, asking yourself questions about it, running over it in your mind, discussing it with someone else, or answering written questions about it. *Stop timing yourself now.*

Now check your new reading speed from the following table. If it is not shown divide 6,000 by the number of seconds you took.

Time in seconds	Reading speed in words per minute
35	171
32	188
30	200
28	214
25	240
23	261
20	300
18	333
15	400
12	500
10	600

This experiment will give you some idea of how with a little effort you can quicken up your speed of reading. What is needed now is regular practice for a few minutes each day to make your new reading speed habitual. *

Are these methods of any value when put into practice? Let the results speak for themselves. For example, a group of banking and industrial employees registered approximately 275 words per minute to begin with. After ten weeks this tempo was increased to 450 words per minute, and the actual comprehension was increased from 45 to 70 per cent of the matter read.

A group of USAF officers increased their reading speed from 292 words per minute to 488 words per minute after six weeks; the slowest officer stepped up his own pace from 106 words per minute to 226 words per minute, and the fastest increased it from 456 words per minute to 810 words per minute.

The question of whether reading speed can be improved without loss of comprehension has been tested experimentally with results which confirm that it can. John Morton of the University of Reading investigated the value of a commercial reading efficiency course. He tested GPO executives, whose ages ranged from twenty-one to sixty-three, before, immediately after and at least six months after the course. He found that their speed of reading was increased but that they understood just as well when they read faster. The mean improvement in reading speed immediately after the course was 64.9 per cent, and even after six months it was still 39.5 per cent. [106]

Paraphrasing Bacon's famous quotation 'Reading maketh a full man,' we may say that 'fast reading makes an efficient man'.

*Further advice and practice materials will be found in the author's book *Rapid Reading* (Thorsons, 1977).

References

(The author gratefully acknowledges his debt to the authors and
    publishers of the works cited in this bibliography.)

1. Dunlop, Erwin. You and your memory. *Psychology*, 1954, 18, No. 3.
2. Barondes, S.H. Some critical variables in studies of the effect of inhibitions of protein synthesis on memory. In Byrne, W.L., ed. *Molecular Approaches to Learning and Memory*. New York: Academic Press, 1970, pp. 27-34.
3. McConnell, J.V. Memory transfer through cannibalism in planarians. *Journal of Neuropsychiatry*, 3 (Supplement 1, 1962), pp. 542-48.
4. Roback, A. A. *History of American Psychology*. New York: Library Publishers, 1952, pp. 365, 362.
5. Heimann, Paula. Certain functions of introjection and projection in early infancy. In Klein, Heimann, Isaacs and Riviere. *Developments in Psycho-analysis*. London: Hogarth Press, 1952, p. 147.
6. Ellson, D. G. Hallucinations produced by sensory conditioning. *Journal of Experimental Psychology*, 1951, 28, 1-20.
7. Baddeley, Alan. *Your Memory: A User's Guide*. London: Sidgwick & Jackson, 1982, p.41.
8. Bartlett, Sir Frederick. *Remembering*. Cambridge: Cambridge University Press, 1968.
9. Di Vesta, F. J., Ingersoll, G., and Sunshine, P. A factor analysis of imagery tests. *Journal of Verbal Learning and Verbal Behaviour*, 1971, 10, 471-479.

10. Baddeley, Alan. *Op.cit.,* p.88.
11. Baddeley, Alan. *The Psychology of Memory.* New York: Basic Books, 1976, pp. 225-6.
12. Baddeley, Alan. *Your Memory: A User's Guide.* London: Sidgwick & Jackson, 1982.
13. Potter, M. C. and Faulconer, B. A. Time to understand pictures and words. *Nature,* 1975, 253, 437-8.
14. Gilbert, J. G. Memory loss in senescence. *Journal of Abnormal and Social Psychology,* 1941, 36, 79.
15. Miles, C. C. and Miles, W. R. The correlation of intelligence scores and chronological age from early to late maturity. *American Journal of Psychology,* 1932, 44, 44-78.
16. Jones, H. E. and Conrad, H.S. The growth and decline of intelligence: A study of a homogenous group between the ages of 10 and 60. *Genetic Psychology Monographs,* 1933, 13, 223-298.
17. Wechsler, D. *The Measurement of Adult Intelligence.* Baltimore, 1944.
18. Werner, H. Development of visuo-motor performance on the marble-board test in mentally retarded children. *Journal of Genetic Psychology,* 1944, 64, 269-279.
19. Gardner, L. P. The learning of low-grade aments. *American Journal of Mental Deficiency,* 1945, 50, 59-80.
20. Miller, Henry Knight. *Practical Psychology.* Marple: Psychology Magazine, 1961, p. 79.
21. Ebbinghaus, H. *Memory.* New York: Columbia University Teachers College, 1913.
22. Gilliland, A. R. The rate of forgetting. *Journal of Educational Psychology,* 1948, 39, 19-26.
23. McGeoch, J. A. and MacDonald, W. T. Meaningful relation and retroactive inhibition. *American Journal of Psychology,* 1931, 43, 579-588.
24. Freud, Sigmund. *Moses and Monotheism.* London: Hogarth Press, 1939.
25. Meltzer, H. Individual differences in forgetting pleasant and unpleasant experiences. *Journal of Educational Psychology,* 1930, 21, 399-409.
26. McGranahan, D. V. A critical and experimental study of repression. *Journal of Abnormal and Social Psychology,* 1940, 35, 212-225.

27. Diven, K. Certain determinants in the conditioning of anxiety reactions. *Journal of Psychology*, 1937, 3, 291-308. Cited in Lundin, Robert W. *Personality: An Experimental Approach.* New York: Macmillan, 1961, pp. 276-277.

28. Blum, G. S. *Psychoanalytic Theories of Personality.* New York: McGraw-Hill, 1953.

29. Zeller, A. F. An experimental analogue of repression. I. Historical summary. *Psychol. Bulletin*, 1950, 47, 39-51.

30. Taylor, Charles and Combs, Arthur W. Self-acceptance and adjustment. *Journal of Consulting Psychology*, 1952, 16, 89-91. Reprinted in Dulany, DeValois, Beardslee and Winterbottom. *Contributions to Modern Psychology.* New York: Oxford University Press, 1958, pp. 269-273.

31. Thompson, George G. and Witryol, Sam L. Adult recall of unpleasant experiences during three periods of childhood. *Journal of Genetic Psychology*, 1948, 72, 111-123.

32. Allport, G. W. *Personality: A Psychological Interpretation.* New York: Holt, 1937.

33. Freud, Sigmund. Leonardo da Vinci and a memory of his childhood. London: Hogarth Press, Vol. XI, pp. 84-85.

34. Freud, Sigmund. *Psychopathology of Everyday Life.* London: Benn, 1948, Part XII.

35. Desmond, Shaw, *Reincarnation for Everyman.* London: Rider, 1950.

36. Freud, Sigmund. *Op. Cit.* Part X.

37. Crönholm, B. Post-ECT amnesias in the pathology of memory. In Talland, A. and Waugh, N., eds. *The Pathology of Memory.* New York: Academic Press, 1969, pp. 81-89.

38. Jacobsen, E. *Progressive Relaxation.* Chicago: University of Chicago Press, 1938.

39. Courts, F. A. Relations between experimentally induced muscular tension and memorization. *Journal of Experimental Psychology*, 1939, 25, 235-256. Cited in Hilgard, Ernest R. *Introduction to Psychology.* London: Methuen, 1957, p. 11.

40. Freud, Sigmund. *Inhibitions, Symptoms and Anxiety.* London: Hogarth Press, 1936, p. 77.

41. Wiksell, Wesley. The relationship between reading difficulties and psychological adjustment. *Journal of Educational Research*, 1948, 41, 557-558.

42. Mursell, James L. *Streamline Your Mind.* London: Watts, 1954.

43. Cantril, H., and Allport, G. W. *The Psychology of Radio.* New York: Harper, 1935, pp. 196-200. Quoted in Abelson, Herbert I. *Persuasion.* London: Crosby Lockwood, 1960, p. 47.

44. Ebbinghaus, H. *Op. cit.*

45. Miller, Henry Knight. *Op. cit.*

46. Katona, G. *Organizing and Memorizing.* New York: Columbia University Press, 1940, pp. 188-189.

47. Ebbinghaus, H. *Op. cit.*

48. Fraser, John Munro. *Psychology.* London: Pitman, 1951, p. 147.

49. Aveling, Francis. *Directing Mental Energy.* London, p. 94.

50. Lorge, I. Influence of regularly interpolated time intervals on subsequent learning. *Teachers' College Contributions to Education,* No. 438.

51. Snoddy, G. S. Evidence for a universal shock factor in learning. *Journal of Experimental Psychology,* 1945, 35, 403-417.

52. Gates, A. I. Recitation as a factor in memorizing. *Archives of Psychology,* 1917, 7, No. 40.

53. Hovland, C. I., Lumsdaine, A. A., and Sheffield, F. D. *Experiments on Mass Communication.* Princeton University Press, 1949, pp. 288 ff. Quoted in Hovland, C. I., Janis, I. L., and Kelley, H. H. *Communication and Persuasion.* Yale University Press, 1963, p. 217.

54. Forlano, G. School learning with various methods of practice and rewards. *Teachers' College Contributions to Education,* 1936, No. 688.

55. Seibert, L. C. A series of experiments on the learning of French vocabulary. *Johns Hopkins University Studies in Education,* 1932, No. 18.

56. Dainow, Morley. *Personal Psychology.* London: Pitman, 1935, p. 103.

57. Krueger, W. C. F. The effect of overlearning on retention. *Journal of Experimental Psychology,* 1929, 12, 71-78.

58. Krueger, W.C.F. Further studies in overlearning. *Journal of Experimental Psychology,* 1930, 13, 152-163.

59. Seibert, L. C. *Op. cit.*

60. Keller, F. S. Studies in international morse code. I. A new method of teaching code reception. *Journal of Applied Psychology,* 1943, 27, 407-415.

61. Fisher, S., and Cleveland, S. E. *Body Image and Personality*. New York: Van Nostrand, 1958, p. 9.

62. Atkinson, William Walker. *Your Mind and How to Use It*. Holyoke, Mass.: The Elizabeth Towne Co.; London: Fowler, 1911, pp. 59-61.

63. Chase, Stuart. *Guides to Straight Thinking*. London: Phoenix House, 1959, p. 34.

64. Freud, Sigmund. Letter to Martha Bernays, Oct. 31, 1883.

65. Thouless, Robert H. *General and Social Psychology*. London: University Tutorial Press, 1937, p. 52.

66. Zeigarnik, B. Das Behalten erledigter und unerledigter Handlungen. *Psychol. Forsch.*, 1927, 9, 1-85.

67. Baddeley, A. D. A Zeigarnik-like effect in the recall of anagram solutions. *Journal of Experimental Psychology*, 1963, 15, 63-64.

68. Ovsiankina, M. Die Wiederaufnahme unterbrochener Handlungen. *Psychologische Forschung*, 1928, 11, 302-379.

69. Marrow, A. J. Goal tensions and recall. *Journal of General Psychology*, 1938, 19, 3-35, 37-64.

70. Atkinson, J. W. *The Projective Measurement of Achievement Motivation*. Unpublished Ph.D. thesis, University of Michigan, 1950. In McClelland, David C. *Groups, Leadership, and Men*. Pittsburgh: Carnegie Press, 1951. Cited in Dulany, DeValois, Beardslee and Winterbottom. *Contributions to Modern Psychology*. New York: Oxford University Press, 1958, p. 225.

71. Rosenzweig, S. Need-persistive and ego-defensive reactions to frustration as demonstrated by an experiment on repression. *Psychological Review*, 1941, 48, 347-349. Cited in Lundin, Robert W. *Personality: An Experimental Approach*. New York: Macmillan, 1961, p. 315.

72. Woodrow, H. The effect of type of training upon transference. *Journal of Educational Psychology*, 1927, 18, 199-272. See Woodworth and Schlosberg, p. 746.

73. Elkonin, D. B. A psychological investigation in an experimental class. *Voprosy Psikhologii*, 1960, 5, 29-40.

74. Jenkins, J. G., and Dallenbach, K. M. Obliviscence during sleep and waking. *American Journal of Psychology*, 1924, 35, 605-612.

75. Johnson, H. M., and Swan, T. H. Sleep. *Psychological Bulletin*, 1930, p.27.

76. Robinson, E. S. Some factors determining the degree of retroactive inhibition. *The Psychological Monographs,* 1920, 28, No. 6.

77. Whitely, P. L. The dependence of learning and recall upon prior intellectual activities. *Journal of Experimental Psychology*, 1927, 10, 489-508.

78. Loewi, O. *From the Workshop of Discoveries.* University of Kansas Press, 1953.

79. Freud, Sigmund. *Introductory Lectures on Psycho-analysis.* London: Allen & Unwin, 1929, pp. 242-243.

80. Freud, Sigmund. *Op. cit.,* p. 92.

81. Reik, Theodor. *The Inner Experience of a Psycho-analyst.* London: Allen & Unwin, 1949.

82. Ferm, Vergilius. Memorizing. In Ferm, Vergilius. *A Dictionary of Pastoral Psychology.* New York: Philosophical Library, 1955, p. 143.

83. Tannenbaum, P. H. Effect of serial position on recall of radio news stories. *J. Quart.*, 1954, 31, 319-323. Quoted in Abelson, Herbert I. *Persuasion.* London: Crosby Lockwood, 1960, pp. 6-7.

84. Thorndike, E. L. *The Fundamentals of Learning.* New York: Columbia University Teachers College, 1932.

85. Krasilshchikova, D. I., and Khokhlachev, E. A. Memorization of foreign words as affected both by the mode of explaining their meaning and by memorization time. *Voprosy Psikhologii,* 1960, 6, 65-74.

86. Boring, Edwin G., Langfeld, Herbert S., and Weld, Harry P. *Foundations of Psychology.* New York: Wiley, 1948.

87. Maddox, Harry. *How to Study.* Newton Abbot: David & Charles, 1970.

88. Andreas, Burton G. *Experimental Psychology*, 1960.

89. Gregg, Vernon. *Human Memory.* London: Methuen, 1975.

90. Baddeley, Alan D. *The Psychology of Memory.* New York: Basic Books, 1976, p. 347.

91. Andreas, Burton G. *Op. cit.*, p. 453.

92. Baddeley, A. D. and Lieberman. Unpublished experiments cited in Baddeley, A. D. *Op. cit.,* p. 230.

93. Bugelski, B. R., Kidd, E., and Segmen, J. Image as a mediator

in one-trial paired-associate learning. *Journal of Experimental Psychology*, 1968, 76, 69-73.

94. Bower, G. H. and Reitman, J. S. Mnemonic elaboration in multilist learning. *Journal of Verbal Learning and Verbal Behaviour*, 1972, 11, 478-485.

95. Laird, Donald A. and Laird, Eleanor C. *Techniques for Efficient Remembering*. New York: McGraw-Hill, 1960, p. 153.

96. Buzan, Tony. *Use Your Head*. London: BBC Ariel Books, 1982.

97. Ballard, P. B. Obliviscence and reminiscence. *British Journal of Psychology, Monograph Supplement*, 1, 2, 1913.

98. McGeoch, G. O. The conditions of reminiscence. *American Journal of Psychology*, 1935, 47, 65-87.

99. Melton, A. W. and Stone, G. R. The retention of serial lists of adjectives over short-time intervals with varying rates of presentation. *Journal of Experimental Psychology*, 1942, 30, 295-310.

100. Freeman, R. *Mastering Study Skills*. London: Macmillan, 1982.

101. Bugelski, B. R. *The Psychology of Learning*. New York: Holt, 1957, p. 311.

102. Hunter, Ian M. L. *Memory Facts and Fallacies*. Harmondsworth: Penguin Books, 1957.

103. Freeman, R. *Op. cit.*

104. Miller, Henry Knight. The ministry of forgetfulness. In *Life Triumphant*. Marple: Psychology Magazine, p. 137.

105. Bayley, Harry. *Quicker Reading*. London: Pitman, 1957, pp. 2, 183, 19.

106. Morton, John. An investigation into the effects of an adult reading efficiency course. *Occupational Psychology*, 1959, 33, 4, 222-237.

Select Bibliography

Avery, Marie L., and Higgins, Alice, *Help Your Child Learn How to Learn* (Prentice-Hall).

Baddeley, A. D., 'Human Memory' in Dodwell, P. C., ed., *New Horizons in Psychology*, Vol. II (Penguin Books, 1972).

——, *The Psychology of Memory* (Basic Books, 1976).

——, *Your Memory A User's Guide* (Sidgwick & Jackson, 1982).

Bransford, J. D., *Human Cognition: Learning, Understanding and Remembering* (Wadsworth, 1979).

Brown, James I., 'Diagnosing Your Reading Problem,' *Modern Medicine,* September 1970.

——, 'Formulas to Improve Reading Efficiency,' *Modern Medicine,* October 1970.

——, 'Purposeful Skimming, Scanning, and Pacing,' *Modern Medicine,* October 1970.

——, 'How to Improve Reading Comprehension,' *Modern Medicine,* November 1970.

Brown, M. E., *Memory Matters* (Sphere Books, 1979).

Burfield, Leone M., 'Rapid Reading and Comprehension,' Lesson 11 in *Effective Speaking and Writing* (Effective Speaking Programme, 1978).

Burnett, Janis, *Successful Study* (Hodder & Stoughton, 1979).

Buzan, Tony, *Speed Memory* (David & Charles, 1976).

——, *Speed Reading* (David & Charles, 1977).

——, *Make the Most of Your Mind* (Pan Books, 1981).

——, *Use Your Head* (BBC Ariel Books, 1982).

Cassie, W. F., and Constantine, T., *Student's Guide to Success* (Macmillan, 1977).

Cermak, L. S., *Human Memory: Research and Theory* (Ronald, 1972).

D'Arcy, P., *Reading for Meaning,* 2 Vols. (Hutchinson Educational, 1973).

Dineen, Jacqueline, *Dynamic Memory Techniques* (Thomas, 1978).

Dudley, Geoffrey A., 'How to Master What You Read,' *The Psychologist Magazine,* January 1974.

——, 'You Can Read Faster and Understand Better,' *The Psychologist Magazine,* April 1975.

——, 'How to Read Faster,' *Memo,* September 1975.

——, *Rapid Reading* (Thorsons, 1977).

Entwistle, N., and Hounsell, D., 'How Students Learn' in *Readings in Higher Education* 1 (University of Lancaster, 1975).

Erasmus, John, *How to Pass Examinations* (Oriel Press, 1979).

Flesch, Rudolf, Witty, Paul, *et al., How You Can Be a Better Student* (Mayflower).

Freeman, R., *Mastering Study Skills* (Macmillan, 1982).

Froe, Otis D., and Lee, Maurice A., *How to Become a Successful Student* (Wilshire).

Furst, Bruno, *Stop Forgetting* (Doubleday, 1972).

——, *The Practical Way to a Better Memory* (R. & W. Heap, 1977).

Furst, Bruno, and Furst, Lotte, *You Can Remember!* (Memory and Concentration Studies, 1977).

Gibbs, G., 'Can Students be Taught How to Study?' in *Higher Education Bulletin,* 5, 2, 1977.

——, *Teaching Students to Learn: A Student-Centred Approach* (Open University Press, 1981).

Gibbs, G., and Northedge, A., 'Helping Students to Understand Their Own Study Methods' in *British Journal of Guidance and Counselling,* 7, 1979.

Gregg, L. W., ed., *Cognition in Learning and Memory* (Wiley, 1972).

Gregg, Vernon, *Human Memory* (Methuen, 1975).

Gruneberg, M. M., Morris, P. E., and Sykes, R. N., eds., *Practical Aspects of Memory* (Academic Press, 1978).

Gruneberg, M. M., and Morris, P. E., eds., *Applied Problems in Memory* (Academic Press, 1979).

Herriot, Peter, *Attributes of Memory* (Methuen, 1974).

Highbee, K. L., *Your Memory: How it Works and How to Improve it* (Prentice-Hall, 1977).

Hill, P. J., *Study to Succeed* (Pan Books, 1973).

Hunt, Ruth C., and Spencer, David G., *Dynamic Reading!* (Rapid Reading Programme).

——, *Reading Improvement Programme* (Rapid Reading Programme).

Jackson, Dennis Barry, *The Examination Secret* (Elliot Right Way Books, 1982).

Katona, G., *Organizing and Memorizing* (Columbia University Press).

Kausler, D. H., *Psychology of Verbal Learning and Memory* (Academic Press, 1974).

Kellett, Michael, *Memory Power* (Sterling, 1980).

Kemble, Bruce, *How to Pass Exams* (Orbach & Chambers, 1980).

Kintsch, W., *Learning, Memory, and Conceptual Processes* (Wiley, 1970).

Klatzky, R. L., *Memory and Awareness* (H. K. Lewis, 1984).

Lorayne, Harry, *How to Develop a Super-Power Memory* (Thomas, 1961).

——, *Remembering People* (W. H. Allen, 1976).

Lorayne, Harry, and Lucas, Jerry, *The Memory Book* (W.H. Allen, 1976).

Lumsden, Robert J., 'Getting More from Your Reading,' Chapter 13 in *Twenty-Three Steps to Success and Achievement* (Thorsons, 1972).

Luria, A. R., *The Mind of a Mnemonist* (Jonathan Cape, 1969).

Maddox, Harry, *How to Study* (David & Charles, 1970).

Main, Alex, *Encouraging Effective Learning: An Approach to Study Counselling* (Scottish Academic Press, 1980).

Mares, Colin, *Efficient Reading* (English Universities Press).

McKeown, Pamela, *Reading: A basic guide for parents and teachers* (Routledge, 1974).

Melton, A. W., and Martin, E., eds., *Coding Processes in Human Memory* (Winston, 1972).

Murdock, B. B., *Human Memory: Theory and Data* (Laurence Erlbaum, 1974).

Neisser, Ulric, *Memory Observed: Remembering in Natural Contexts* (W. H. Freeman, 1982).

Norman, D. A., ed., *Models of Human Memory* (Academic Press, 1970).

——, *Learning and Memory* (H. K. Lewis, 1982).

Orton, J. Louis, *Memory Efficiency and How to Obtain It* (Thorsons).

Parsons, Chris, *How to Study Effectively* (Arrow Books, 1976).

Penry, Jacques, *Looking at Faces and Remembering Them: A Guide to Facial Identification* (Elek Books, 1971).

Philp, Howard L., *Memory: How to Make the Most of It* (Thorsons).

Postman, L., and Keppel, G., eds., *Verbal Learning and Memory* (Penguin Books, 1971).

Rapaport, D., *Emotions and Memory* (International Universities Press).

Reading Centre, *4 Steps to Successful Learning* (Reading Centre, 1975).

Rhodes, Martin, *How to Study* (Thorsons).

Robinson, F. P., *Effective Study* (Harper & Row, 1970).

Rowntree, Derek, *Learn How to Study* (Macdonald, 2nd ed., 1976).

Shone, Ronald, 'Imagery as a Memory Aid,' Chapter 8 in *Creative Visualization* (Thorsons, 1984).

Smith, Nila Banton, *Be a Better Reader* (Prentice-Hall).

Stauffer, Russell G., and Berg, Jean Horton, *Project Learn: Rapid Comprehension Through Effective Reading* (Learn Inc., 1974).

Tulving, E., and Donaldson, W. A., eds., *Organization of Memory* (Academic Press, 1972).

Union of Lancashire & Cheshire Institutes, *Success in Examinations* (ULCI, 1974).

Various, *A Dictionary of Mnemonics* (Eyre Methuen, 1972).

Wainwright, Gordon R., *Rapid Reading Made Simple* (W. H. Allen, 1972).

Weinland, James D., *How to Improve Your Memory* (Barnes & Noble).

Wood, Ernest E., *Mind and Memory Training* (Theosophical Publishing House, 1974).

Yates, Frances A., *The Art of Memory* (Penguin Books, 1978).

Index

action theory, 69
active method, 104
advertising, direct-mail, 37
age and memory, 30, 158
Aitken, A.C., 40
amnesia, infantile, 46
  reasons for, 46
  senile, 44, 51, 158, 159
Andreas, Burton G., 109, 116
Aristotle, 98
ars quadrata, 117-118
  rotunda, 118
assimilation, law of, 101
association, laws of, 98-102, 161
  how to use, 103-105
  value of, 102
Atkinson, J.W., 85
Atkinson, W.W., 81
attention, 60-63
  active and passive, 72
  definition of, 35, 61
  law of, 35, 63, 70
  value of, 63
audiles, 23
autosuggestion, 66, 73, 81, 159, 160
Aveling, Francis, 76

backgammon, 115
Baddeley, A.D., 24, 25, 83, 110, 118
Ballard, P.B., 138
Bartlett, Sir Frederick, 25
belongingness, law of, 74
Bergson, H.L., 151
Berlioz, H., 41
Blum, G.S., 43
Bower, G.H., 122
Bruno, Giordano, 117
Bugelski, B.R., 122, 139
Buxton, Jedediah, 29
Buzan, Tony, 138, 139

Campbell, Judith, 65
Camus, Albert, 33
Chartres Cathedral, 118
Chase, Stuart, 82
Combs, A.W., 43
comprehension, 73-75
concentration, 60-72, 159
  summary of advice on, 71, 72, 159
confabulation, 52

confidence, 81-82
consolidation, 38, 89, 151, 157
contiguity, 99
contrast, 99
Courts, F.A., 69
cryptogram, 123-125

Dallenbach, K.M., 90
Davis, 137
day-dreams, 63
déjà vu, 52-56, 102
  definition of, 52-53
  examples of, 52-56
  explanations of, 53-56
  in dreams, 56
Desmond, Shaw, 53
Dickens, Charles, 53
Dictionary of Pastoral Psychology, A, 99
distortion, 157
disuse, 34, 36-37, 151-152
Doyle, Sir Arthur Conan, 39
Dreams: Their Mysteries Revealed, 93
drugs, 57-58, 159

early memories, 47-51
Ebbinghaus, H., 36, 37, 74, 75
ECT, 57
ego-orientation, 86
eidetic imagery, 22
Elkonin, D.B., 88
emotional conflict, 69-71
essay-type exams, how to answer, 141-143, 164
examinations, 132-149, 163-165
examination technique, 132-149, 163-165
Experimental Psychology, 109

'faculty' psychology, 18-20
falsification, retrospective, 28
fantasy, 51
  unconscious, 56
Faulconer, B.A., 26
Ferm, Vergilius, 99
Field, Shirley Ann, 49
figure and ground, 86
fire risks, 127
Fludd, Robert, 118
forget, how to, 150-155, 165
  summary of hints on, 154-155, 165
forgetting and sleep, 90, 153, 158

forgetting, causes of, 34-59, 60, 150-151, 157-159
  rate of, 36, 157
  summary of practical hints on, 161, 165
Foundations of Psychology, 108
free association, 95-98, 161
  definition of, 95
  examples of, 95-98
Freeman, R., 139
frequency, law of, 100, 101
Freud, S., 41, 46, 47, 52, 55, 70, 83, 86, 95, 96
From the Workshop of Discoveries, 94
Furst, Bruno, 78

General and Social Psychology, 83
generalization, principle of, 101
Gilbert, J.G., 30
Gilliland, A.R., 37
Goethe, 47, 48
Green Cross code, 110
Gregg, Vernon, 109
Guides to Straight Thinking, 82

habit, 63
habit memory, 20, 156
hallucination, 22
Hawthorne, Nathaniel, 27
history dates, 113
Hood, Thomas, 43
Hound of the Baskervilles, The, 39
How to Study, 108
Human Memory, 109
Hunter, Ian M.L., 139
Hyden, 16

idiot savant, 29
imagery, problems with, 24-27, 156
imagination, 15, 156
immediate memory, 21
impression, 60-73
  weak, 35-36, 46, 151
inhibition, proactive, 39, 40, 152-154, 158, 161
  retroactive, 38, 152-154, 157, 161
Inner Experience of a Psycho-Analyst, The, 96
inspiration, 93
intelligence and memory, 28-30, 156
intensity, law of, 100

intention to remember, 72, 73
interest, 65-68, 163
interference, 34, 38-41, 152-154, 157-159
  avoiding, 89-91
Introductory Lectures on Psycho-Analysis, 96

Jacobsen, E., 68
James, William, 15, 64
Janet, P., 40
Jenkins, J.G., 90
Johnson, 90

Kidd, E., 122
Korsakoff syndrome, 52

language study, 82-83, 103, 104
law of reversed effort, 92
letter places, 123-131, 162
  in learning, 125-131, 163
Lewin, Kurt, 84
Lieberman, 118
Life Triumphant, 150
'little and often', 75-77, 160
loci, 116-131, 162
Loewi, O., 94
logical memory, 21
Luria, A.R., 31

McConnell, J.V., 17
McGeoch, J.A., 138
Maddox, Harry, 108, 109
Mah Jong, 115-116
marijuana, 58, 159
Mastering Study Skills, 139
matrix, 129, 130
meaning, memory and, 73-75
Melton, A.W., 138
memorizing, 27-28
memory and age, 30, 158
  and intelligence, 28-30, 156
  benefits of, 30-33
Memory Facts and Fallacies, 139
memory for completed and uncompleted tasks, 83-86, 160
memory images, types of, 22-24
memory, is it a 'faculty'?, 18-20
memory optimists, 43-45
  pessimists, 43-45
memory span, 21
memory trace, 15, 34, 36, 38, 89, 151, 156
  energy of, 34
memory, types of, 20-22
memory, what is it?, 15-33, 156
Metrodorus, 117
Miles, C.C., 30
Miles, W.R., 30
Miller, Henry Knight, 35, 74, 150, 151, 152
mnemonics, 108-131, 162-163
  devise your own, 112-113, 162
  elaborative, 112, 162
  reductive, 112, 162
  simple, 110-111, 162
  types of, 111-113, 162
Moore, 137

Morse code, 80, 113-114
motiles, 23
Muensterberg, 69

names, remembering, 79
notes, how to learn, 135-137, 163
  how to take, 134-135, 163
  purposes of, 134

olfactory memory, 24
'one-word' translation, 103
Open University Foundation Courses, 128-131
Outsider, The, 33
overlearning, 73, 78-80, 160
Ovsiankina, M., 84

Paradise Lost, 147
phonetic alphabet, 78
Pitman shorthand, 39
place memory, 116-131, 162
  applications of, 118-131
Potter, M.C., 26
Practical Psychology, 35, 74
'practice makes perfect', 101
predominant mental impression, law of, 35
proactive inhibition, 39, 40, 152-154, 158, 161
problems solved in sleep, 93
Progressive Relaxation, 68
Psychology of Memory, The, 110
pure memory, 20, 156
P-V formula, 163-164

random access, 118, 162
reading and rereading, 135, 160
recalling, 27
recall, methods of, 91-98
recency, law of, 44, 100
recitation, 73, 77-78, 160
  reasons for, 77
Reik, T., 96
reincarnation, 53, 54
Reincarnation for Everyman, 53
reintegration, 73, 82, 83, 94, 160
  examples of, 94-95
Reitman, J.S., 122
relaxation, 68-69
remember, how to, 60-107, 159-165
  intention to, 72, 73
remembering, definition of, 15, 156
  summary of practical hints on, 156-165
  the English counties, 105
  theories of, 16-18
  ways of, 27-28
reminiscence, 138, 139
remote memory, 21
repetition, 73-88, 160
  conditions under which effective, 73-88, 160-161
  experimental proof of value of, 73
repression, 35, 41, 46, 86, 91-93, 154-155, 158, 159, 161-162, 165
  and maladjustment, 43
  definition of, 41

experimental proofs of, 42-43
  methods of relieving, 91-98, 161-162
  reasons for, 41-42
retention, 28
retroactive inhibition, 38, 152-154, 157, 161
revision, 137-140, 164
Roback, A.A., 19, 20
Robinson, E.S., 54
Rosenzweig, S., 85
rote memory, 21
Royal Horses, 65
Rule of Health, 117

Science and the Paranormal, 17
screen memories, 47
scriptural texts, memorizing, 81
Segmen, J., 122
Seibert, L.C., 80
shock, 56-57, 159
Shute, Nevil, 28
similarity, 99, 152, 158
Simonides, 117
Singer, Barry, 17
skill, acquiring, 76, 77
'sleeping on it', 93, 161, 165
smoking, 58-59, 159
spaced learning, 73, 75-77, 160
speech, how to remember, 106-107
'spotting' exam questions, 148-149
Stone, G.R., 138
style of life, 48-51
Swan, 90

Tacitus, 104
tactiles, 24
task-orientation, 86
Taylor, C., 43
tension, 68-69
terms of reference, 141, 142, 143-147
'thingummybob' principle, 15
thinking, 15, 156
Thompson, G.G., 45
Thorndike, E.L., 101
Thouless, R.H., 69, 83
Town Like Alice, A, 28

Use Your Head, 138

visiles, 23
vividness, law of, 100, 153
von Restorff effect, 86

whole learning, 73, 80-81, 160
Witryol, S.L., 45
word places, 120-122, 162
  square, 123-125, 162
worry, 69-71

Young Goodman Brown, 27

Zeigarnik effect, 74, 83-86, 160
  illustrations of, 84-86
  reversal of, 85, 160
Zeller, A.F., 43
zoology, 120-122